KNOWING WHY
Adult-Diagnosed Autistic People on Life and Autism

Edited by
Elizabeth Bartmess

The Autistic Press

WASHINGTON, DC

Edited by Elizabeth Bartmess
Front Cover Design by Amythest Schaber

ISBN: 978-1-938800-07-8
Library of Congress Control Number: 2018954422

Printed in the United States of America

Dedication

To all the people who never had a chance to know they were autistic because they lived in the wrong time or place,

and to all the people who will come to learn they're autistic but have yet to join us.

We hold you in our hearts.

CONTENTS

INTRODUCTION

ELIZABETH BARTMESS

You may have picked this book up because you suspect you're autistic, or know you are, or are just beginning to wonder whether you might be. You may have a formal diagnosis, or be self-diagnosed. You may have only recently learned you're autistic, or you may have known for a long time.

Or you might be what the autistic community has in the past called an "autistic cousin": someone who shares significant similarities with autistic people due to cerebral palsy, or hydrocephalus, or ADHD, or some other reason. Or you might not be autistic or an autistic cousin; you might be trying to educate yourself so you can better understand a friend or family member who recently learned they're autistic.

If you're tentatively wondering whether you might be autistic and are wondering whether it's "okay" for you to read this book: it is. It's okay to explore and learn about yourself and other people. You're not hurting anyone by learning about what it's like to be autistic. You are actually *helping* us by reading what we have to say about ourselves in our own words. I mention this because I have known so many autistic people who were afraid that considering they might be autistic would somehow harm others—perhaps because we have so often been told we are selfish for saying we have needs and experiences that differ from other people's, or because we have been told that exploring our similarities is appropriation (it is not).

This writers in this anthology are all autistic people who first learned they were autistic as adults, either via formal diagnosis or via self-diagnosis after research and much thought.

Sometimes, as Erin Human discusses in the first piece in this anthology, people ask why it's important to know you're autistic, if you've made it to adulthood without knowing. Often, by the time we learn we are autistic, our needs have gone unmet for so long we are in burnout or crisis. Even when we're not, we've often spent decades struggling with aspects of life that seem effortless for others. If we've lucked into a series of particularly supportive environments, we may not have needed to know—but that isn't common, and it is better for us to learn we are autistic *before* before entering a new, potentially less friendly environment.

Much of what we struggle with come from others misidentifying our needs and differences. For example, when someone interprets our executive function difficulties as laziness, our difficulty interpreting social cues as maliciousness, our sensory sensitivities as pickiness, or our difficulty with eye contact as disrespect, they are likely to mistreat us—especially if our explanations are then treated as evidence that we can't be trusted to report accurately on our own experiences. To avert some of that mistreatment, we often spend major effort to appear more superficially "normal," which can be necessary, but passing (or attempting to pass) as neurotypical in this way carries its own kind of damage.

Learning we are autistic helps us begin to address some of the accumulated costs of being so often misunderstood—costs that can be emotional, social, financial, educational. Once we know we're autistic, we can make better sense of our lives, connect with other autistic people, and gain knowledge and coping skills. We can process sadness, anger, or grief over a life that could have been different with more support. If formally diagnosed, we may also be able to access accommodations for school or work, or apply for disability assistance. Not all of us seek or receive a formal diagnosis; the advantages of a formal diagnosis are inaccessible to people who can't afford one, or who don't have access to a provider knowledgeable about what autism can look like in adults, or who risk losing child custody or employment if diagnosed. And some people may choose not to pursue a formal diagnosis if they don't think it would be helpful to them personally. But the advantages of *knowing* we are autistic are available to everyone.

This anthology is part of a larger conversation going on among autistic people and sometimes autistic cousins. It takes place in many places: in small groups, at disability and autism conferences, over IM and text messages, on bulletin boards, on social media, over email, in person. (Sometimes it even takes place on the phone.)

It has been going on for a *long* time. Autistic people have met each other by chance and talked about our similarities and differences since before the diagnosis existed, but having a label to describe ourselves makes a big difference. And the internet has amplified everything by bringing together geographically distributed people and providing text-based ways to communicate that help many of us with auditory processing issues, anxiety, or difficulty speaking.

This conversation, in all its forms and venues, helps us come to know ourselves not just individually but collectively. We talk about our similarities and differences, build a knowledge base, and try to support each other. We take what we learn back into our lives, and often into the broader world as well, through self-advocacy and activism in school, at work, or in public life.

The title of this anthology, "Knowing Why," comes from A.J. Odasso's piece about passions and growing up autistic: "You spend a lot of time wondering what's wrong without ever knowing why." The value of knowing *why* we are different from so many other people, why it can be so hard to do things others can take for granted, and why there is often such a mismatch between others' treatment of us and our own needs, skills, and experiences, is a common part of this larger conversation, and it is reflected throughout this anthology.

The authors in this anthology have written about personal experiences that connect to issues common among autistic people, particularly adult-diagnosed or self-diagnosed autistic people. They have often included practical suggestions.

This anthology includes pieces on a number of themes:

Burnout

Many adult autistic people come to a diagnosis or self-diagnosis due to burnout—a period when, after many years of struggling to cope, the demands of everyday life become increasingly difficult or impossible. Erin Human writes about her experiences with going into and climbing out of burnout, and discusses why burnout happens, why remedies designed for neurotypical people don't always work for us, what can help, and why knowing that you are autistic can be a necessary first step toward recovering.

Passions

Many of us have passions (often referred to as special interests)— topics or activities that we find especially compelling, interesting, or rewarding. They can play important roles in our sense of self, in developing a sense of skill, in helping us recover from stress and burnout, and, not least, in providing us with entertainment and joy. A.J. Odasso writes about growing up undiagnosed, their passion for knowing the names of things from a very early age, and the role that exploring passions can play in self-understanding and in emotional stability.

Sensory issues and social spaces

Many autistic people have differences in sensory perception. Noises, sounds, textures, or other sensory input unremarkable to others can be painful or aversive to us. We may also have more difficulty noticing some sensory input. Stuart Neilson writes about how his diagnosis explained many previously puzzling difficulties he'd had, describes coping strategies, and talks about how sensory issues can influence our ability to handle social situations. He also discusses how some of the difficulties we encounter are due to deliberate choices in the design of public spaces—which could instead be designed in sensory-friendly ways.

Working while autistic

Gaining, keeping, and coping with employment is difficult for many of us, for many reasons, including those related to sensory, social, and executive function. Kelly Bron Johnson writes about her experience with being employed and the range of issues that learning she was autistic helped with, including overcommitment, hyperfocus, sensory sensitivities, diplomacy and office politics, communication, accommodations, and learning to recognize when to leave a job.

Intersecting identities

Many of us, in addition to being autistic, are members of other marginalized groups. We may wind up spending a lot of time asking ourselves why people respond to us as they do—whether it is due to being autistic, or to something else, such as being black, or queer, or physically disabled—without being able to achieve a definitive answer. This can complicate our relationship to autistic communities—which, depending on where we are, may assume that we don't differ from the Western cultural "default" of being white, cishet, physically abled, middle-class, male, etc. It can also complicate our relationship to communities focused on other identities, which may assume that we are neurotypical. Morénike Giwa Onaiwu writes on intersectionality[i], describing multiple situations in which she's struggled with wondering whether something—poor treatment by restaurant staff or store owners, underestimation of academic and cognitive ability, or something else—happened to her or her children because they are autistic, because they are black, or for some other reason. She concludes with a point that is worth emphasizing: communities, resources, solutions, etc., shouldn't require us to parcel ourselves up into pieces; being autistic is not something we can separate off from other parts of our identity. Knowing that we are autistic can be essential; dividing our identity up into discrete pieces should not ever be necessary.

Identities, coping skills, and community

Skills we learn for interfacing with the world with respect to other identities can help with being autistic, and vice versa—and identity-based communities can be testing grounds for new skills. Samantha Hack writes about her experiences with being autistic, transfeminine, and physically disabled, how skills gained for one of these can help with others, and how she uses her accepting queer and autistic communities to pilot new skills. It is also common for autistic people to be gender non-conforming in various ways, including being transgender and/or nonbinary, something which has received increasing attention in recent years, and Samantha's discussion of her experience with gender and transitioning will be of interest to many readers.

Healthcare, chronic illness, and mental illness

While navigating the healthcare system can be difficult for anyone, it can be particularly challenging for autistic people. Health professionals can respond with unwarranted suspiciousness, and sometimes open mistreatment, to our ways of communicating and our accommodation needs, and often lack knowledge or are misinformed about autism and common co-conditions such as sensory processing disorder. Amythest Schaber writes about her experiences with seeking healthcare for chronic illness and mental illness, and what she has learned along the way.

Depression

Depression is a common issue for autistic people, contributed to by social isolation and abuse, as well as other common issues such as poverty, unemployment, and stress. We also often struggle with the guilt, self-blame, and confusion that can come with not knowing why we have the difficulties we do. In a set of four related autobiographical stories, M. Kelter writes about his experiences with depression, family, and growing up undiagnosed. In "The Lamp," he describes something very common: Aiming for a neurotypical life won't fix depression; pressure from others to do so doesn't help. "Beekeeper," a story about an interaction with a relative with similar autistic traits, shows how passions can create social connections. In "Oubliette," he describes how isolation and social pressure can lead to feeling broken and withdrawing. In "Red Ledger," he shows how having a supportive person can help, talks more about the pain of family being oblivious to childhood isolation and depression, and concludes that "confusion and self-doubt and uncertainty about [his] own nature," for him, as for many of us, are major contributors to discomfort around others—one reason that knowing we are autistic is so important.

Technology

The anthology ends with a look at current technology and at our cultural future. Many of us use technology to support communication, socialization, organization, motor skills, and safety, among other things. A.C. Buchanan writes about their own experiences with technology as an autistic, dyspraxic person, including the reasons that helpful technology should not require a diagnosis to access and the ways people sometimes treat our technology use as "wrong." They close by raising questions for discussion about the relationships between technology, self-image, and autistic culture.

Before closing, a quick note: we have not standardized international spellings, or asked contributors to use specific language to refer to themselves. You will see English from the U.S., Canada, New Zealand, and Ireland in here. Most authors refer to themselves as autistic; some reference the autism spectrum or Asperger syndrome (which, while no longer a separate diagnosis in the U.S., continues to be in use in some countries, such as the U.K.).

There's a saying that if you know one autistic person, you know one autistic person. We share similarities and differences with each other and with autistic cousins. If you are autistic, or an autistic cousin, you may see your experiences reflected in many of these pieces. It is also possible that you won't. Similarly, if you are reading to better understand an autistic friend or family member, you may find some of the pieces in here helpful, but it is good to keep in mind that the autistic person you know may not have had any specific experience you read about.

It is very common for autistic people—including people who have been professionally diagnosed—to doubt whether they are autistic. Many of us have learned, for safety reasons, to habitually scan social environments for indicators of whether we are safe and welcome, or will need to leave. This often extends to identity and group membership, especially when we have been treated as unreliable narrators of our own experiences and pushed to not trust our own perceptions and self-knowledge. We may have been shamed for thinking, or acting, like we have something in common with autistic or other disabled people. Our experiences with chronically attempting to conceal our differences may have left us with a fear of being exposed as not genuine. This can leave us simultaneously excited to read about people who may be like us, and afraid we will find out we don't belong. If you feel this way, you may want to do something calming before moving on—find a quiet place, or something to fidget with, or put on some comforting music. It may also help to remember that this anthology is an offering of experiences and tips, some of which may be relevant to you and some not; you are free to find them useful or not, and you do not have to be autistic, or an autistic cousin, to use a suggestion or idea from in here that is helpful to you.

If you are exploring whether you might be autistic, or are autistic and have not interacted with other autistic people much, or are an autistic cousin who is comfortable doing so, I would like to invite you, after reading this book, to join in our larger conversation. I have included a list of recommended resources at the back of this book to help you find online or in-person spaces.

Regardless of who you are or where you are coming from, I hope that you will find something useful in here. One of the tricks to being autistic, or an autistic cousin, is to make space in the world where we can be comfortable. I hope you find things in here that will help you to create—or shore up, or expand—such a space for yourself.

ABOUT THE EDITOR

Elizabeth Bartmess is a Bay Area writer, editor, and autistic advocate. She runs weekly Twitter chats for autistic people and autistic cousins (hashtag: #AutChat; website: http://AutChat.com) and has written about autistic representation in fiction. She also writes humorous science fiction and fantasy and is a graduate of the 2016 Clarion West writers workshop. You can find her on Twitter at @theoriesofminds; her website is http://elizabethbartmess.com.

---

[i] Intersectionality is a term created by civil rights advocate and critical race theory scholar Kimberlé Crenshaw in 1989 to describe an approach to understanding an individual's overlapping social identities as not distinct and separable, but an intersection that creates qualitatively different experiences from having just one identity, or a different combination of identities. See Kimberlé Crenshaw, "Demarginalizing the Intersection of Race and Sex: A Black Feminist Critique of Antidiscrimination Doctrine, Feminist Theory and Antiracist Politics", *University of Chicago Legal Forum* (1989), 140:139-167.

EMERGING FROM BURNOUT

Erin Human

When I think of burnout I flash back to a memory. I am sitting on my kitchen floor, my body wedged into the doorway. My back pressed against one side of the frame, my feet braced against the other, afternoon sun keening through the blinds, and I am crying. Because I'm so tired. I've just carried a load of laundry down to the basement and walked back up the stairs and I don't know how I'm going to make it through the rest of this day.

Like so many other autistic people I've talked to, burnout was the catalyst for my self-identification. I didn't know what was happening to me, but I knew that I was not okay anymore. I had done all the usual things a person is supposed to do when they don't feel right—seen my doctor for a full physical exam, made efforts to improve my diet, added vitamin supplements. I was doing my best to get enough sleep (as much as a parent of two young children can). I had mood trackers on my phone, meditation tracks I listened to stretched out in a dark bedroom after dinner while my husband played with the kids. I read books, I wrote a blog, I was seeing friends in person at least once a week, I tried yoga, I took walks, and still—

I was not okay, anymore.

I was lucky, in a sense, because some people crash much harder when they burn out. I did not end up hospitalized, physically ill, or stranded in a major depressive episode. But in another sense this made it tricky to get the supports I needed to pull myself out of burnout, because it never felt like a crisis in need of immediate help. It just felt like I was in a stripped down survival mode, every day. All I could see in front of me was making it to the end of that one day.

But I reached a point when I had heard myself say, "I'm sorry, I'm just so tired" to my children enough times that I knew I couldn't go on like that. Thus began the process of climbing out. All in all, it took two years, and plenty of trial and error. And the very first step I had to take was realizing that I was autistic.

People often wonder what the point is of identifying oneself as autistic in adulthood. The way they see it is, you've made it this far, what difference does it make now? What they don't understand is how autistic people like me have only made it that far by clawing our way there, by struggling in silence, by turning ourselves inside out, and we can't do it anymore. My story is a common one: the adult autistic who pushes themselves too far beyond or outside the boundaries of their neurological makeup, for too long, in order to keep up with the demands of a neurotypical lifestyle, will eventually burn out. And that's when we will finally seek the answer to a question that's been at the back of our minds for most of our lives: exactly *why* am I different from those other people?

All humans have a kind of personal economy of well-being in which certain things (sleep, food, enjoyment of personal hobbies/interests) replenish us and others deplete us (stress, illness, hunger, sleep deprivation). That's not unique to being autistic, but because our environments are so often ill-suited to our needs, autistic people are more likely than neurotypicals to run on a deficit for extended periods of time. When we have to cope on a regular basis with sensory overload or sensory deprivation, social situations that confound our natural abilities, and executive functioning demands with too little support, we are living beyond our means. When other pressures are added to those—such as a high stress job or schooling, illness, lack of sleep, poor nutrition, financial strain, dysfunctional family relationships, and so on—burnout is almost inevitable.

Reaching the state of burnout can happen quickly in a high stress environment, or it can in some cases be an incredibly slow slide. In my case, burnout crept up on me almost imperceptibly.

I had been that autistic girl who flies so smoothly under the radar that even she doesn't know she's not like the other kids at school. I certainly felt different from everyone around me, but I tended to brush off the differences as superficial; things I could "overcome" or grow out of or at the very least hide. As a child of a certain age it was important to me to fit in, but later I was compelled to suppress my differences simply in order to get by—to achieve, to pass, to get the A, get the job, get the paycheck, and on it went. I dismissed my particular needs as personal weaknesses and did my best to ignore or somehow "fix" the things about me that I thought made me *less than* other people—less socially adept, less comfortable in my skin, less confident, less competent. I wanted to be more like other people—not because I disliked myself, but because I perceived that others moved through the world with so much more ease than I did; I assumed it must be something about *them*, rather than something about the world, that smoothed the roads before them while mine was so rough, uphill, and littered with unexpected pitfalls.

Over time I cultivated a habit of working against my own neurology, fighting with it and trying to twist my nature into something more...well, normal. Even though I felt myself to be trying harder than most people had to try, just to do the most ordinary things of life, I convinced myself that all that held me back from doing better, being better, and feeling better, was that I just had to try a little harder.

And that's what gradually led me to crumple onto my kitchen floor in tears, defeated by a single, lowly load of laundry at the age of thirty-five.

Everything changed for me when a Facebook friend shared a blog post they'd read about having intense sensory issues during the changes in season. It was October, and as I read the post from the blog *Musings of an Aspie* (https://musingsofanaspie.com/), I was overwhelmed by a feeling of familiarity. Intrigued, I read another post on the blog. Then another, and another. And I kept thinking, *this is me*. I continued to read, searching for more autistic bloggers, poring through their archives, especially if they were women—their life experiences, thoughts, and feelings resonated with me like nothing I'd ever read before. I'd been a lifelong bookworm, always searching for an image of myself in the novels and memoirs I read, but never quite finding my reflection, until I read the words of other autistic people.

I started my own Facebook group for women and nonbinary people who thought they might be autistic (and a few who were sure they were), and together we explored what that meant to us. In each other we finally found other people who could answer, "yes, I feel that way too," so we could begin to understand who we really were. Though I would eventually pursue and obtain a formal diagnosis, it was then and it still is the community of other autistic people that is the most vital part of my sense of autistic identity. No doctor's paperwork can compare to the feeling of belonging and mutual understanding that I feel among my autistic friends.

Realizing that I was an autistic person grappling with burnout was the key step to recovery, but it was only one step. The process of figuring out what would actually help me feel better, conserve and restore my energy, and prevent me from tumbling into burnout in the future, was experimental. I tried some things that worked and many more that failed. When you are autistic and grappling with burnout and you set out to seek help, you will find that many of the techniques recommended to neurotypical people dealing with burnout or depression do not work for us. Sometimes they can even make burnout worse or send us into shame spirals over not being able to do the things that we've been told will make us feel better.

I've found this to be particularly true as an autistic woman, and I'm sure the same goes for anyone else commonly perceived to be female—we're often told that what we need is to get out more, do more social get-togethers, have more date nights if we have partners, hire more babysitters if we have children. And though human connection can be a balm to the soul for anyone, in-person social engagements require a heap of executive functioning and social energy expenditure that can leave autistic people more depleted than before. Before I knew better ways to do autistic self-care, I tended to pile more outings and social events onto my plate and then feel like a failure when I crashed and had to hide in my house for weeks just to recover from all the "fun" I'd been having.

Along the same lines, neurotypical women often find comfort in various beauty and body care treatments that may or may not work for autistic people. Some of us might love a visit to the hairdresser, a mani-pedi, a massage, but for many others one or all of those things are sensory nightmares—and, not to mention, financially inaccessible for quite a few disabled people. One person who was trying to help me asked when was the last time I spent time in a hair salon: well, I started cutting my own hair over a decade ago when I couldn't afford a pro cut, and I've never stopped, because making small talk with a hairdresser is one of the most exhausting things I can imagine.

Another relaxation method that didn't work out for me is meditation, suggested by a former therapist. For a few months I dutifully stretched out in my bed in the dark each evening, with headphones on and a guided meditation track playing in my ears. I would spend twenty minutes adjusting the seams on my sleeves and pondering whether to do something about the light beaming in from the hallway through the crack of the doorway, and afterwards I'd get up refreshed—no, I'd get up thoroughly irritated and craving a break from all that mindfulness. I've been surprised at how many autistic people I've chatted with who have had similar experiences with meditation, and I wonder if this is because of the way the autistic mind experiences the sensory world. Perhaps for us, to focus our attention on the present moment means that we let in a rush of unfiltered sensory information that is simply too much to endure... Certainly, I did not find it particularly relaxing!

Perhaps the most frustrating part of autistic burnout is the constant brain fog: the feeling of not being able to hold a train of thought for any length of time, the memory loss, the inability to access words whether spoken or typed, finding a blank slate where your visual thinking used to readily supply images. As an artist, I was sad to have lost my creativity when I burned out. I missed the swirling activity of my fractally-thinking autistic brain in better days.

So if it's not meditation, what tool do autistic people have for resting and restoring our minds? Eventually I found it: deep focus. This is one of my favorite parts about being autistic and one of my most reliable support strategies. When I am in deep focus, the sensory world dims to a comfortable backdrop, the brain fog lifts, and I can reconnect to that wordless sense of self that makes me feel all is right in the world, for a time. Every autistic person has their own pathway to deep focus—it might be drawing, reading, gaming, knitting, singing, Lego building or spending time with animals. Mine happens to be making graphics on my computer, a deeply satisfying activity that stimulates my visual brain and reboots my creative energy.

For autistic people to practice good self-care that works and doesn't end up feeling like more work than rest, we may have to do a lot of trial and error—though I am hoping that over time we will build up our own cultural database of self-care strategies. The more we talk to each other about what works and what doesn't, the more we can learn about ourselves.

One of my self-care discoveries was that playing loud music in my headphones or in my car is calming—even better if I can sing along. I've talked to several autistic people who agree that this is an effective remedy for overload—though it may seem counterintuitive that loud music could be the antidote to the stress caused by a noisy, distracting environment, it works for many of us.

When getting together in person with other people is too much, connecting online is often a better alternative for autistic people. And because the noise of social media can be overwhelming and stressful, we have workarounds for that—like using the Groups app for Facebook, where you can still access the groups you use to chat with friends but not have to see everyone's political views on your main timeline. Other group text chat apps like Slack, Line, Skype, or Google Hangouts are common coping tools that I use and my autistic friends also use when we want to stay connected but need to scale down our consumption of media and public social spaces.

Exercise is another common prescription for dealing with depression, anxiety, or burnout, but again autistic people might need to think outside the box to find the avenues that get our bodies moving in ways that actually do nourish us instead of wearing us out further. Running the treadmill at a busy gym full of people and their sounds and smells might be one of the worst ways I can think of to spend my time, and I would rather die than ever take a Zumba class. But I love doing home improvement projects, painting and re-painting rooms, cleaning out the garage, trimming my fruit trees and pulling weeds. I have autistic friends who enjoy gardening, rock climbing, martial arts, hiking.

So much of surviving as an autistic person has to do with sensory self-care. Sensory processing challenges seem to be something that most people associate more with autistic children, but of course adults still experience the sensory world in ways that can affect our energy levels, moods, and ability to thrive. For most of my life I had not made the connection between my near constant low energy levels and near constant auditory overload, but once I recognized it, I could make sense of why I feel so drained in many environments.

Having hyperacusis (heightened sensitivity to certain frequencies and volumes of sound, common among autistics) means that the sound of a crowd of people, heavy street traffic, a blaring television, or echoey acoustics in a room, will send me quite rapidly into sensory overload. If I can't get away from such an environment promptly, my mind and body will both begin to shut down, my physical energy depleted as well as my abilities to think, listen, and talk. Now that I'm aware of this, I know that I need to have auditory supports available to me almost all of the time (noise canceling headphones or earbuds, foam earplugs will do in a pinch), and sometimes I may need to escape the environment altogether.

I often have somewhat delayed interoception, meaning that I may not realize I am hungry or tired or cold or hot until I am so hungry/tired/cold/hot that I am on the very brink of a breakdown. This is another area where self-knowledge is the key to self-care; checking in with myself periodically to assess whether I have unmet body needs can avoid a lot of misery later.

One of the most important adjustments that I've had to make in my life to find my way out of burnout has been to reduce the number and intensity of demands on myself—in other words, to do *less*. It's a simple concept but so hard to practice for those of us who have made a lifestyle out of overcompensation. A friend once described me as "ambitious," which surprised me at the time, but I've come to understand that being driven and perfectionistic are adaptations I have devised to cope with having an invisible (and until recently unidentified) disability.

But those adaptations have come at a price—a vicious cycle of pushing myself until I crash and then pushing harder still. I'm learning to build more downtime into my life, but it's a challenge. When I'm not "productive" (according to my own harsh standards), I struggle with guilt and a wilting sense of self worth. I often have to remind myself that this attitude is actually ableism, embedded deep in my thoughts—that I would never be so hard on an autistic friend as I am on myself. It's taken me some time to really understand and accept that being disabled is real. That I *am* disabled, in fact. And that trying just a little harder to somehow *not* be disabled is exactly what got me in over my head in the first place.

As I've slowly but surely emerged from burnout over the past two years, I've regained so much of my energy, my creativity, and my optimism. This restoration comes with a risk, as finding myself capable of once again driving toward productivity, I'm tempted to do it. To push myself to achieve and to win the kinds of accolades that have seduced me throughout my life. I catch myself saying yes to more things, looking for busy-ness to fill up my days now that I have some energy to spare, and sometimes I realize with a sinking feeling that I have promised more than I can deliver. These old habits are hard to kick, but at least now I have a roadmap to follow and before I get totally lost. I recognize the signs of overdoing it earlier; I know why I need to stay in my pajamas all day after spending half a day socializing; I bring my noise canceling earbuds with me everywhere. I remind myself over and over again that *being disabled is real.*

ABOUT THE AUTHOR

Erin Human is an autistic parent of two children. She grew up in New England and studied illustration at Rhode Island School of Design before graduating from Marlboro College in Vermont with a degree in Art and Writing. She and her spouse moved to Omaha, Nebraska in 2006. Erin works as a self-employed artist creating graphics, cartoons, and writing on her website about being autistic, parenting, homeschooling, and other topics of interest. Her passions include reading, writing, drawing, social media, alternative education, and the neurodiversity movement.

You can find her website at https://erinhuman.com and her Facebook at http://www.facebook.com/theeisforerin.

BEING THE DICTIONARY: ON PASSIONS, DIAGNOSIS, AND INTEGRATION

A.J. ODASSO

When I was a child, I tended to think of myself as a person who knew what I liked.

More specifically, I thought of myself as someone whose likes and dislikes were so pronounced that there were only two ways in which anyone my own age could possibly react to me: with a sense of almost immediate kinship, or with an attitude of cruel disdain. My experience of friendship, particularly from kindergarten through junior high, fell consistently along those lines. At any given time, I had only two or three close companions; meanwhile, the remainder of my peers either ignored, teased, or outright tormented me. Looking back, I'm consistently surprised at the lack of in-between.

I spent a lot of time thinking about the things I liked, mostly because I had the keen desire to work out what was so objectionable about my interests. Aside from my parents, teachers, and the occasional slightly older child who'd show me kindness, I preferred to be left alone. I preferred to read: cryptozoology books, ghost stories, Shakespeare, and YA novels I'd later learn to classify as speculative fiction. Preferred to sit alone in a particular seat at the front of the bus, right-hand side when facing the front, and watch the same scenery pass day by day: one montage on the way to school, one on the way home. I'd compose lyrics in my head, sometimes linked to melodies and sometimes not; I'd later classify it as poetry and start writing them down. I had a keen interest in the flora of Pennsylvania, the state in which I grew up, so I'd spend recess at the edges of the playground, wandering as far as I could, collecting and naming specimens. I worked out how to crack hickory nuts without damaging the meat.

My interest in learning the names of things in the world has been with me for as long as I can remember. I was an early talker; from eight months, I knew the alphabet, and my first words—*What's that?*—had been nontraditional, if telling. By the age of two or three, I'd memorized the names of an entire set of Pennsylvania Game Commission *Fish of North America* flashcards. I also knew the names and specifications of most popularly-known dinosaurs by heart, and even a handful of obscure ones.

The names of things, *specificity*, mattered to me more than it seemed to matter to most other people I knew, and it was puzzling. It's the only lens through which I can explain how literacy—grammar, spelling, syntax, and all the rest—came to me as easy as breathing.

I was three-going-on-four the day words on a page first snapped into focus. I read them out as loud as I could so that my mother in the kitchen could hear. She responded kindly, but dismissively, saying it was a book she'd read me so many times that I'd surely just memorized them. Angry, I set down the Disney hardback adaptation of *Dumbo* and grabbed a book at random off the shelf. I read part of a sentence to prove I wasn't faking. I'll treasure her amazement as long as I live.

Sadly, much of my life since has been similarly devoted to convincing others I'm not an unreliable narrator. Even though I was considered less socially inept by high school (and even regularly had more friends to boot), I was still surrounded by the same children who'd been tauntingly calling me The Dictionary since grade-school. From first grade on, I'd earned that particular reputation from my consistently error-free weekly spelling tests and the fact that, during games of hangman and similar, I could frequently guess the puzzle with only one or two letters in place.

Being the dictionary is only helpful when other kids want you on their team so that they'll earn more points when the puzzle's guessed with a maximum amount of blanks. Similarly, it's only helpful in adult contexts when your weirdly specific skills and knowledge-sets can benefit those around you in a far more complex way. You spend a lot of time wondering what's wrong without ever knowing why—and, for someone who values specificity? It produces the worst anxiety you can imagine.

Even though I'd worked out how to guess at social cues (with variable results, granted) and even managed to muddle my way through a couple of two-year-long serious relationships by the end of college, I didn't feel any closer to actually understanding why most people seemed to tire of me before I'd really gotten to know them, or why people seemed to think nothing of excluding me by lies of omission, or why I couldn't pay attention to a dozen things at once for purposes of accomplishing tasks like driving or playing the piano (no matter how hard I practiced) or socializing at crowded parties.

I still preferred the company of names, of fascinating things in the world, of *words*. I learned with the advent of universal internet access that my ideal medium for communication, for initial connection, was through written correspondence and chat interfaces. Long before I ever worked up the courage to start submitting my poems to journals, I learned that there was an audience for the stories I liked to tell. What's more, I learned that I told them *well*. For once, my knowledge and skill-sets weren't a means to an end. They were tools I used to create art that contained not only characters and worlds worth getting lost in, but conveyed something of *who I was*.

My diagnosis of Asperger's/autism didn't arrive until the summer of 2014. An unrelenting series of traumatic events between late 2010 and early 2012 had exacerbated my long-established tendencies toward anxiety and depression to such a point that borderline-suicidal stress meltdowns were a several-times-weekly, if not daily, occurrence.

At the time, I was working in a high-pressure environment for a major university where my superiors—that is, I effectively had three bosses at once—seemed to believe I'd intuit their meaning from what were, to me, intolerably vague instructions surrounding complex documentation procedures. Although I'd invariably work out my own shortcuts and yield efficient results, I was constantly called on my unorthodox approaches to workflow and my lack of hesitation to ask blunt questions.

Six months in, I was afraid I'd lose my job even though I'd been giving it my all.

I'd been in therapy since 2012, and to mixed results. I cycled through two or three practitioners to extreme dissatisfaction; none of them seemed to ask questions beyond *How do you feel today?* or follow-ups like *Why do you think that is?* Their lack of specificity disturbed me. I wanted to say: *If I knew, I'd surely tell you. Isn't it your job to direct these encounters to get to the bottom of things?*

The most recent of those three failed therapists was the one to refer me for neuropsychological testing, and the result, delivered kindly-but-severely, was an eye-opener. And it reminded me of something: a friend-of-a-friend in the UK had once candidly asked me when I'd found out I was autistic. I'd simply blinked at her, too shocked to respond. She'd said it was all right, that my mannerisms and way of taking things in reminded her of her daughter. At the time of that conversation, I was twenty-seven, and the friend-of-a-friend's daughter was around eight or nine.

Receiving an autism spectrum diagnosis six months before my thirty-third birthday was not something I'd been expecting, but it didn't come as the shock you might expect. The data I'd accrued for years, viewed through this filter, made a startling amount of sense. Not everyone is prepared for exchanges as intense and earnest as the ones I prefer. Not everyone sees hyperfocus to the exclusion of nearly all else as a strength. Not everyone considers encyclopedic memory an advantage, and not everyone regards passion for forms of writing that aren't guaranteed to earn a fortune as admirable.

What I've come to realize is that most people seem to like an exhausting array of things in a general sense, whereas I love a specific and carefully-curated array of things with all my heart. And while I've had to engage in a voracious amount of exploratory reading and conversations with other autistic people, as well as in trial-and-error analysis of thirty-six years' worth of data, I always come back to the things I love best. Those, I know as well as I know myself, and the secret I've discovered is that they contain, in and of themselves, endless new themes and variations.

My advice to you—especially if you are a newly-diagnosed individual or someone questioning and seeking diagnosis, whether self-determined or professional—is to discover that secret. By this, I mean that you should examine as much of your accrued sense of self as you possibly can, whether the time at your disposal has been eighteen years or eighty, and search for patterns. What are your interests, and why do you take pride in them? Why do they bring you pleasure, or a sense of security, or whatever benefit it is that they happen to bring you? How do these pursuits help you to feel more secure in who you are, and how do you feel about yourself when you have the chance to share them with others?

Ultimately, my primary interests, over time, have made their way into my writing. I'm a published poet and writer of short fiction, as well as a university-level educator and departmental editor for a major SF/F/Spec magazine (*Strange Horizons*, http://strangehorizons.com). I've discovered that sharing my passions in writing, whether as prose or verse, has the dual benefit of keeping me emotionally stable—writing as a primary form of stimming, if you will, as I started using an old typewriter at a very young age because I loved the feel and sound of the keys—and permitting me to share what I've learned and experienced via means I find more intuitive than verbal exchange.

Creative pursuits in conjunction with regular therapy sessions have, ultimately, proved the most effective means by which I've been able to integrate my diagnosis into my sense of self. Over time, it's become less a thing that I've discovered and more a thing that I've known all along, but for which I lacked frame of reference and vocabulary. Written language has been my key to acceptance and understanding; however, you may discover that, for you, it's something else. I have autistic friends for whom computer programming, painting, and even welding have been keys to self-understanding.

One thing that autistic people seem to have in common, at least in my experience of having quite a number of close friends who are also on the spectrum, is that we're system-builders. This is often expressed in terms of routine being important to us, although, as we're well aware, that's not universally true. We construct systems, whether entirely of thought or by using some combination of thought and external manifestation, that help us to interpret data the world throws at us and also to find our place in relation to it. Scripting is an excellent example of one such system, and whether you were taught what scripting was or felt your own way into it (as I did, through years of writing), it's a perfectly valid means by which some autistic people choose to interact with the world.

For me, diagnosis has been a piece of information that needed to find a place in my scripting system. When and how, in telling my story to others, do I include it? *Should* I include it? Are there circumstances in which including it could do me more harm than good? Are there circumstances in which *omitting* it could do me more harm than good? Not everyone will find this to be the case, but I've actually discovered that I feel more secure, in most circumstances, when I include it. Where I previously might have encountered massive misunderstandings (like the ones that once led to the anxiety that I might lose my job), I've found that people generally show a willingness to be more open-minded and accommodating. As a result, my style of communication comes off as less of a shock.

Of course, diagnosis also results in a new set of challenges. Increased instances of ableism are inevitable. I've been told more than once, on first meeting someone and disclosing my diagnosis, that "[they] never would have guessed [I was] autistic" or "don't worry, [they] never would have been able to tell." And while people who make statements like these often mean well, it's never helpful; it can be painfully invalidating after how long and difficult the road to diagnosis has been. I've learned to view these encounters as a chance to educate others, although not all of us have the time, energy, or ability to do so. Acknowledging the limits of what you can handle, knowing what's safe, is vitally important.

Lastly, on a related point, integration of diagnosis into self-knowledge has meant learning not to let others make me feel ashamed of who I am. As difficult as facing the aforementioned type of person (or even those who still feel compelled to outright mock and belittle) can be, taking pride in my autistic identity in much the same way that I take pride in my writing has been both empowering and necessary. I would not be the editor, educator, or writer that I am if I was not *exactly the way I am*. I understand now that my neurotype is as inseparable from my creative output as it was from the so-called weird kid with strong preferences that I was over twenty years ago. The weird kid's grown up, that's all, and learned to put those strong preferences to creative use. Knowledge is as productive as it is powerful.

A final caution, especially for those who can be as impatient as I am: it won't all make sense overnight. I was diagnosed in 2014, but I'm still working my way through a number of residual challenges. Aside from one sister who's a graduate student in psychology, my family has been slow to understand the implications. One parent wondered if they were to blame, based on a harmful and outdated theory that's been disproved many times over, and the other has often erred on the side of assuming I'll never achieve my full potential because the "issue" has been explicitly brought to light.

The difficulty of communicating and educating, I've found, is amplified when the people in question are ones who have known and cared about you for years. They don't want to believe something is "wrong" with you; given that they're prone to framing it in such terms, they'll often attempt to assign blame, to discover a root cause, or may even begin to patronize you. I have found framing myself in terms of my disability to loved ones far more tricky than I believe it should be, when these individuals have (in theory) known who I am, *the way I am*, for my entire life.

Similarly, navigating romantic relationships, even long-term ones, may become more of a challenge. My partner of eleven years left me four years after some revelations about my biology and how it relates to my gender identity, and only two years after my autism spectrum diagnosis. It was during this four-year period that they grew progressively selfish, snappish, and withdrawn. The more empowered I felt in my increasingly nuanced self-knowledge, the more insensitive my partner became. You may find that your partner, instead of supporting you, will do the same. As reprehensible as such actions are, it's important to remember that the flaw lies not with you, but with them.

As viewpoint-altering as all of this might sound, the end result of the challenges I've faced in the past few years, particularly the ones relating to my diagnosis, is that I'm unshakeable in my belief that acceptance begins with discovery. Learn everything you can about yourself; search memories and consider past experiences valuable sources of information. When push comes to shove, nobody knows you better than you know yourself. If you seek professional diagnosis, you will very likely be asked to give a personal history either verbally or in writing; I didn't know this going into the process, and I wish that I had. It would have been a less stressful verbal recounting if I'd had the chance to review myself and script it ahead of time. The psychologist who diagnosed me said my intake appointment took almost twice as long as it should have because I consistently missed her subtle cues that I should move on from one phase of my life to the next. From my point of view, I was just being thorough!

Unfortunately, chances are high that you will be told time and again, often by people you love and trust, that you're an unreliable narrator, that your perceptions can't possibly be trusted. Chances are also high that academic and professional colleagues will try their level best to discredit you, no matter how well you perform your job. These are only a small fraction of the challenges we face in a world that's ultimately not designed for us, in spite of the fact that we have a hand in building it. Our plans and contributions are consistently dismantled and swept aside. This is what I work to change.

Whether you arrive at self-knowledge via professional means or self-determined ones, know this: your diagnosis is valid. *You* are valid. The systems you build for purposes of interacting with the world are valid. There is nothing about your experience as an autistic person that is not valid.

(*What's that?* is still the first question I always ask, the better to determine what I like.)

ABOUT THE AUTHOR

A.J. Odasso's poetry has appeared in a variety of publications, including *Sybil's Garage, Mythic Delirium, Midnight Echo, Not One of Us, Dreams & Nightmares, Goblin Fruit, Strange Horizon*s, *Stone Telling, Farrago's Wainscot, Liminality, Battersea Review, Barking Sycamores*, and *New England Review of Books*. A.J.'s début collection, *Lost Books* (Flipped Eye Publishing), was nominated for the 2010 London New Poetry Award and was also a finalist for the 2010/2011 People's Book Prize. Their second collection with Flipped Eye, *The Dishonesty of Dreams*, was released in 2014; their third-collection manuscript, *Things Being What They Are*, was shortlisted for the 2017 Sexton Prize. They hold an M.F.A. in Creative Writing from Boston University, where they were a 2015-16 Teaching Fellow, and work at the University of New Mexico. A.J. has served in the Poetry Department at *Strange Horizons* (http://strangehorizons. com) since July 2012. You can find them on Twitter at @ajodasso.

SENSORY ISSUES AND SOCIAL INCLUSION

Stuart Neilson

1. Late diagnosed Asperger syndrome in Ireland

I am a late arrival to autism, diagnosed seven years ago at the age of forty-five. I had a lengthy history of mental health issues up until then that, rather suddenly, were "better explained" by Asperger syndrome than any of the labels that psychiatry had failed to cure me of. It was a turning point in my life because I suddenly discovered a working set of explanations for almost all of the issues I'd struggled with throughout my life. Most of these had previously been identified within someone else's authoritarian and "expert" framework: as educational failure, problem behaviour, mental illness or social dysfunction. I have had plenty of advice over many years on how I should buck up, pull myself together and just try to fit in. Equally suddenly after diagnosis, I now realised that many of the issues that affect me on a day-to-day basis and determine the quality and extent of my social life are fundamentally sensory differences. I feel that I have a limited supply of "Social Calories" that I can either use up gradually in extended, relaxed social activities or burn rapidly in high-pressure social settings, after which I need some alone time to recover. I consume Social Calories faster when sensory distractions and social interaction compete for my limited attention.

At school I was called a dunce (and made to stand in the corner at the front of the class wearing a conical hat with a "D" on it) and I was warned that I would be sent to a school for the educationally-subnormal (an ESN school, in the expert educational language of the 1970s, or more commonly "a school for dummies" among my classmates). I failed the 11-Plus, a kind of IQ selection test for ability-streamed secondary schools that some politicians are keen to bring back. Despite this, I also had flashes of genius, alternated between "A" grades and failures, and had the bitter-sweet nickname of "egg-head." I don't think that I will ever finish my education because I enjoy learning too much to stop and because I am an unemployed and relatively unemployable middle-aged autistic adult with a history of mental illness. My highest qualification is currently a doctorate in statistical modelling—so much for school experts and selective exams.

When we talk about the senses we usually talk about the obvious five external senses of sight, sound, touch, smell and taste that we use to perceive the environment. We also have a less discussed range of internal senses for perceiving our own balance; the position of our body parts; and our heartbeat, temperature, and digestive states. Some of these internal states are strongly related to states of emotional arousal. My own senses are heightened with respect to certain kinds of distracting noise, visual movement, and unexpected skin contact. I have an extreme dislike of some textures that verges on phobia. I am not particularly sensitive to my balance, body position, temperature, or bladder and bowel fullness. This individual profile differs from other people diagnosed with the same label, but I have found a comforting sense of community in knowing that other people with my label also have heightened and diminished sensory perceptions as compared with the neurotypical majority.

Interestingly, my sensory issues are more difficult in social contexts. I love listening to a tree full of rowdy crows cawing, flapping, and diving between branches. A barn full of cows and steaming dung brings me a warm sense of calm, no matter how noisy the cattle. Even the synthetic cacophony of machinery is sometimes a delight—I could easily spend hours watching Industrial Revolution exhibitions of belt-driven weaving machines tracing the same mesmerising patterns over and over, until my family eventually drags me away. My musical tastes are very diverse when I am alone, but I might find the same music intolerable in a crowd. Being at one with and engaged in the sensory world, rather than having the burden of sensory distractions on top of social demands, seems to be a key factor in whether sensory experiences are positive or negative.

The analogy of Social Calories has helped me understand that there are situations, always with a social component, that I find very draining. I often feel the need to sleep through the day after a party, lecture, or social gathering. Many other people seem to thrive on social interaction and to build up their positive energies in the exact settings that sap mine. Being able to identify the impact of different kinds of social interaction on my energy allows me to choose how and when to engage, and when I need to take time out to recharge. I believe that we are all social animals and I do desperately crave social connection, but I am not well-equipped to find social connections that are fulfilling without exhaustion. Breezy gossip, polite small-talk, social competition, workplace joshing, and second-guessing other people's unspoken subtexts are all particularly hard. It is a search for settings where, to parallel the DSM-5's description of autism, "social demands do not exceed limited capacities"[ii]—settings where the rewards of contact with other people exceed the energy (and sometimes the pain) of engaging with them.

With the benefit of four decades of hindsight I can easily identify how sensory issues helped to create the genius-dummy schoolchild with my (then) unpredictable mixture of social withdrawal and extreme chattering. I am shocked that modern schools, with far more hindsight at their disposal, still fail to recognise the role of sensory differences even now. I never got the hang of any physical sports, especially team sports, and my fear of being touched affects me in almost any public place to this day. I usually overdress in both summer and winter to keep my skin protected from unexpected light brushes and I am very picky about fabrics and hygiene products touching my skin, though I recently discovered a range of soft T-shirts that vastly expands the range of clothing I can wear without being distracted by the textures. Security staff have been called to help control my outbursts when doctors and others have touched me in unexpected ways (a hint: just say *what* you are going to touch, in simple words, *before* you touch it).

2. My knowledge and lack of understanding

I used to believe that I had a reasonable knowledge of what autism is, but after diagnosis, realised that knowledge and understanding are very different things. I had known a number of autistic adults when I was in school, at a time when autism was rarely diagnosed and the label "Asperger syndrome" did not exist. I also have a number of younger relatives whose autism was recognised while they were in school. These two groups of people are very diverse, they are not obviously like each other and they don't share any obvious character-istics with me. I had also, like everyone else, seen various Hollywood interpretations of autism in the form of films such as *Rain Man* and *Mercury Rising*—which again are very diverse and share little obvi-ous in common with the autistic adults I knew, or with younger au-tistic people, or with me. I did have one fleeting sense of self-recog-nition with a character in an episode of the Australian hospital drama *All Saints*, who is told that his patterns of rigid thinking and inflexible routine place him "on the same spectrum" as his autistic son. There is really no other screen portrayal of autism that I strongly identify with, but there are a number of characters in fictional books, where I suppose some degree of imagination helps me see myself in their portrayal.

In short, I was unable to locate cohesive and consistent features connecting these very different real and fictional characters. I was unable to recognize any shared common elements of their characters, behaviours and lives that could bind them together under the single umbrella of autism. It was only much later, well after my own diagnosis and self-research that I have been able to see the threads that connect very different expressions of shared autistic features. Context, the quality and availability of social relationships, verbal expression, and so many other individual and environmental factors lead to very different expressions of underlying autistic traits, such as those related to social interaction and communication and so-called "restrictive and repetitive behaviours." With fictional characters, authorial and editorial decisions can result in inaccurate or obscured portrayals of autistic traits—fiction and film are intended to entertain a primarily neurotypical audience, and not to educate.

Bullying and a sense of social isolation have been difficulties throughout my life, especially during school. These two problems became especially severe in a new job after moving to Ireland, where I experienced a level of workplace bullying and harassment that led to clinical depression and anxiety. I ended up in the public mental health system and went through a number of diagnostic labels and a long series of different prescription drugs, at one point being labelled with "treatment resistant" symptoms. One psychologist eventually recognised that some of the "symptoms," such as my limited outward expression of emotional reactions and distractable attention, were innate characteristics and not something that could (or should) be cured.

I was extremely lucky in being in the public health system, where a multidisciplinary assessment and diagnosis were accessible, and lucky to be under the care of the psychologist who proposed the assessment. Adults over eighteen years of age in Ireland do not have easy access to assessment and some people even have difficulty in obtaining a referral to a psychologist or psychiatrist. Private assessment is expensive and some people offering private assessment are not qualified, so their diagnostic reports are not always accepted when accessing services. My psychologist did not impose the assessment and outcome on me, but instead asked me if I knew anything about the autism spectrum (which of course I claimed to know plenty about) and then suggested that I go home, read up some more about adult autism, discuss it with my family and then tell him at the next appointment whether I would like to pursue an assessment and possible diagnosis. I was extremely surprised that anyone would suggest autism (which I knew about) was relevant to my difficulties, although my family were not in the least surprised.

3. My lightbulb moments

Some autistic people may reject a professional evaluation and diagnosis as personally meaningful because they don't feel a formal affirmation would further their understanding of autism or its relation to themselves, but in my own case (where I had never even considered a connection) it has been a vital self-awakening. The formal diagnosis has also been a key, rightly or wrongly, to services that are only available to adults who have been formally diagnosed by a registered psychologist or psychiatrist. For me, diagnosis was my "light bulb moment" in which many difficult or puzzling aspects of my life suddenly made sense.

I have often felt a sense of guilt over clumsy and uncomfortable social interactions, where I come away with a sense of having failed. Over a lifetime, I have internalised a deep sense of shame in social settings. Sometimes I find that although I have heard people clearly, I can't immediately understand the meaning of the sounds they made, and have no way to respond to them. Afterwards I am able to recall the sounds, as if playing the whole interaction back again, and kick myself for having missed even simple conversations. In reality I have been feeling anxiety and discomfort that other people probably did not notice or paid little attention to, and I have internalised my discomfort and feelings of stupidity as shame. In that sense autism is a "Not Guilty Verdict" for a lifelong feeling of social isolation.

Most importantly for me, the sensory issues of autism explain a great deal of my difficulty in navigating shared public places and social groups, and even explain some food intolerances. I find social interaction much harder in large, busy places, becoming irritable and uncommunicative even with my immediate family. The same factors become more bearable in a computer superstore or museum that interests me. Noisy social gatherings make me nervous, especially with strangers or in strange places, but are more bearable if the event is something with formal structure such as a religious occasion. One lifelong mystery had been illness after eating baklava, but not after eating kataifi, even though both are pastry sweets made from the same basic ingredients; baklava is served at weddings and other events with high sensory and social demands, but kataifi is eaten at home. I also have a strange fondness for styles of beat-driven music that I use when working, but would never listen to for pleasure. These paradoxes begin to make sense when taking into account how autistic sensory sensitivities can differ by context.

The words "autism" and "Asperger syndrome" open up access to a vast array of books and internet pages (some of which are extremely misleading and occasionally harmful) and to both virtual and real life communities of autistic people. I have seen dispute within the these communities, which is especially bitter between autism organisations and groups, as well as long-running arguments over the "correct" labels for autistic people. I tend to agree with Judy Rapoport's statement "I am incredibly disciplined in the diagnostic classifications in my research, but in my private practice, I'll call a kid a zebra if it will get him the educational services I think he needs."[iii] Precision is helpful from a scientific and statistical perspective, but real life requires elasticity. I reject blatantly false labels ("sufferer" is one of the worst), but have a relaxed attitude to other labels, so long as they are technically accurate and used with good intent.

4. Public spaces and sensory issues

There is a retail phenomenon called (in a tragic irony) the Gruen Effect in which sensory disorientation and sensory confusion can be deliberately engineered in a shopping mall to create uncertainty and anxiety in shoppers. The response of most people is to resolve their anxiety by transferring all their uncertainties into shopping, with an easy resolution (literally) staring them in the face. It is a tragic irony because the Austrian architect Victor Gruen, who designed the first indoor, air-conditioned shopping mall at Southdale, Minnesota, in 1956, was a fierce critic of the "bastard developments"[iv] that became a total opposite to his original intentions. Gruen wanted to integrate safe retail, work, and suburban environments, to prioritize pedestrian traffic, to reduce commuting time, and to foster a real sense of community. For people who don't receive a sense of certainty and fulfilment from impulse shopping, the modern shopping mall is an experience of extreme discomfort that only obstructs carefully planned purchases.

Public spaces like shopping malls, offices and airports make me far more nervous than most people. I am aware now (since diagnosis) that my discomfort is not all caused by people staring at me, or being angry with me, or thinking about me in unkind words like "weirdo" that have been so familiar since childhood. A large part of my discomfort is caused by sensory overload and sensory distraction that has been deliberately designed into many public spaces. Simply being aware of the source of that lifelong discomfort is enough to be able to participate in a wider range of everyday activities than I have in the past.

It is really important to note that public spaces like these are the result of a design *choice* to create uncomfortable environments, and not a necessity. That choice may be because my sensory comfort is expensive to accommodate, or because most people actually *like* the disorienting public environments we have available, or at least spend more time and money on them.

I do occasionally attract the attention of suspicious security staff who notice me because I am not behaving in the way they expect of a typical shopper, office worker or passenger. Air travel has become a special circle of hell with the modern theatre of security, which is designed to comfort travellers through the illusion of greater safety. Airline organisations have developed formal systems to pick out weird behaviour (like mine) along with genuine security threats. The most publicly exposed system is the leaked TSA "Screening of Passengers by Observation Techniques" (SPOT) Referral Report[v], although air travel worldwide presumably operates similar behavioural screening programmes. The SPOT screening test counts up the number of suspicious behaviours such as avoiding eye contact, fidgeting, hand-wringing, a cold stare, appearing to be confused, or not responding to verbal requests. If passengers score four or more points-worth of suspicious behaviours then they are selected for additional scrutiny or a law enforcement officer is called over to assess them for potential threat. The behavioural screening checklist reads very much like a diagnostic test for differences in sensory perception. Needless to say, I (and one of my children, who is autistic) are more often picked out for a rigorous search and extra interview questions than either other people we travel with or other passengers.

When I travel I now carry a photo ID card that identifies my diagnosis, along with a first-responder information leaflet with a brief guide to autism and Asperger syndrome. I have never presented the ID card, but it is a comfort to know I do have it if I ever need to explain my behaviour—it amazes me how language evaporates into incoherence or silence when I am anxious. I once spent an hour undergoing an enhanced security inspection at Bristol airport, with body searches and inspectors opening the seams in my baggage, which might have been quicker if I had been able to retain my usual verbal fluency and answer the security questions more fully.

5. Managing my sensory sensitivities

I have not found it easy or comfortable to start thinking of myself as "a disabled person," but I am very conscious of having to contend with many disabling environments. There are disabling places in which my capacity to function is reduced by the architectural design or the sensory ambience. I am comfortable in identifying my own impairments (in medical language) and the processes by which they interact with certain environments to disable me. This is consistent with the Social Model of Disability, which contends that disability is not innate and is not the inevitable consequence of impairment. Disablement is the systematic oppression and exclusion of people with impaired functions from mainstream society, through social and economic processes as well as through the infrastructure and architecture we are forced to navigate if we wish to be full participants in society. "Impaired function" is not always a limitation in itself, but becomes limiting when it conflicts with a world designed for "normal" levels of function. Shopping malls, airports, and inconsiderate working environments are all examples of the social and economic choices by which society excludes autistic people from full participation.

It is easy to avoid sensory distress by not going out, but avoiding sensory distress comes with an opportunity penalty, including fewer friendship, educational, and job opportunities. There are ways to be less uncomfortable in a world structured by and for people who do not experience distress at continuous, varying noise and light. Most people seem to be positively energized by sensory loads and seem to equate the "buzz" of a noisy shopping mall or café with their image of personal economic and social success.

My hearing is probably my most impaired (or least conforming) sense, and I find many noises intrusive, distracting or painful. Noises that have a high energy output in a narrow frequency range (such as sirens, beeping cash tills, or piped music) are the worst. I find that a thick, woolly hat comfortably muffles noise and I am lucky to live in a climate that excuses wearing a hat almost all year round. At home I use noise-cancelling headphones to electronically reduce external noise, as well as noise-isolating earbuds to exclude external noise. These devices reduce external noise rather than masking it with music, which can harm hearing when used to simply raise the overall sound level. I have never been comfortable in public wearing headphones because I am too old to be cool, but I have mapped out a collection of quiet, dim safety corners in shops where I can take a time-out if I get stressed or anxious while shopping. The technical, bookkeeping, and computer science sections of bookshops are a frequent oasis of calm.

Flashing lights and cheaply-made LED lighting systems (which visibly flicker, especially in peripheral vision) are an annoyance, but become a more serious problem when combined with noise. Christmas is a particularly hard time because not only shops but the entire street-scape fill with synchronised musical light displays, leaving very little opportunity to escape. It is not necessary to rebrand everyday provisions in festive pictures and sleigh bells, but somebody in the marketing department must find it desirable. Shopping earlier in the day and away from busy centres is usually quieter. Shopping for clothes is always hard (a one-size-fits-all uniform in one colour would suit me just fine, eliminating all that anxiety-inducing choice) but clothes shops tend to be calmer on the days when big sporting events have kept all the other potential shoppers away watching the game.

I often say (usually in inappropriate settings) that there are only two common activities that simultaneously engage all five external senses: food and sex. Some less common activities such as painting, pottery or gardening can evoke strong flavours if you happen to lick a stained finger or use your lips to bring the tip of a paintbrush to a point. Any of these might be either pleasant or horrible, depending on the activity, the context, and whether the contact was intentional or expected. Just having advance warning of a sensory experience can be enough to convert an unpleasant sensation into a bearable or pleasurable event. Some public spaces do manage to engage the senses of taste and odour either deliberately with perfumes (think of candle shops) or inadvertently with airborne dust. Building works often release dust that has a strong flavour and odour. Coffee-grinders and similar machines also release flavour into the air.

GPS and hand-held mapping have transformed the way I feel about travel and my rigid belief that there is *only one right way* and every other turn is the *wrong way*. I have never learnt to drive, but the calm voice of the GPS soothes me because it is always capable of recalculating a new route and showing how every point on Earth is connected to the destination, no matter which turns the driver takes. I am now a much less anxious bad passenger. We use a "Smartie trail" process to mark out key points in holidays and journeys—the timing is not critical, so long as the next Smartie (a meal break, a museum or a hotel) is foreseeable. Our family also structures the anxiety-provoking unknowns of a strange place into a set of building blocks by highlighting the enjoyable things to see or do in a tourist information brochure, or collecting a list of things we might do from internet searches, without necessarily timetabling each and every hour. We know each of the building blocks, and don't need to know their order or what the final building will look like. It is easy to find internet images of most places, or even to rehearse an entire journey in a street view before visiting. Anticipating a collection of future experiences is much more pleasant than fearing unstructured days in a strange place.

There have been some wonderful developments in "autism-friendly" and "sensory aware" public initiatives in recent years. These include autism awareness training amongst airport and airline staff; autism-friendly sessions in many museums, cinemas, and theatres; and autism-friendly shopping hours in supermarkets. At their best, these initiatives take place in normal business hours and require no passport to entry, meaning that nobody polices or questions any diagnosis or other reason for using the facility, which is simply available to all potential customers. The most effective of these initiatives are directed by people who are intimately familiar with the experience of autism. Two that are worth a special mention are the Royal Collection Trust, which has fabulously detailed guides on the sensory and anxiety experiences of visiting the royal palaces in London, and the availability of autism-friendly shopping in Supervalu Supermarkets in Ireland, with reduced visual and auditory distractions in a weekly time slot. The best initiatives are motivated by or consistent with the Social Model of Disability, clearly locating the problem of disablement within the environment and not within the person.

The focus of autism has always been on children and the undoubted importance of early intervention, but the most important message I have learned is that people are always capable of learning, at any age. There is no age point after which intervention is worthless or support is no longer valuable. I have learned a great deal in the way of useful strategies to participate in society and I have unlearned some limiting sensory avoidance techniques that avoided positive engagement with other people. There is a great deal that can be achieved by the three quarters of autistic people who are adults.

ABOUT THE AUTHOR

Stuart Neilson lectures and writes about the autism spectrum as a health statistician and from his personal perspective of an Asperger syndrome diagnosis in 2009, at the age of forty-five. He was a founder member of the team that developed the innovative Diploma in Autism Studies at University College Cork, Ireland. He has a degree in computer science and a doctorate in mathematical modeling of inherent susceptibility to fatal disease. Stuart Neilson's most recent books include *Living with Asperger syndrome and Autism in Ireland*, *Painted Lorries of Pakistan*, and *MND Essentials: Your Fifty Key Questions Answered*.

[ii] "Symptoms must be present in the early developmental period (but may not become fully manifest until social demands exceed limited capacities, or may be masked by learned strategies in later life)." American Psychiatric Association, "Neurodevelopmental disorders", in *Diagnostic and Statistical Manual of Mental Disorders*, 5th ed (Arlington, VA: American Psychiatric Association Publishing, 2013), doi:10.1176/appi.books.9780890425596.dsm01.

[iii] Judy Rapoport, quoted in Arthur Allen, "The Autism Numbers", *Slate*, January 15 2007, http://www.slate.com/articles/health_and_science/medical_examiner/2007/01/the_autism_numbers.html.

[iv] Victor Gruen, quoted in Anne Quito, "The father of the American shopping mall hated what he created," *Quartz*, July 17, 2015, https://qz.com/454214/the-father-of-the-american-shopping-mall-hated-cars-and-suburban-sprawl/.

[v] Jana Winter and Cora Currier, "Exclusive: TSA's Secret Behavior Checklist to Spot Terrorists," *The Intercept*, March 27, 2015, https://theintercept.com/2015/03/27/revealed-tsas-closely-held-behavior-checklist-spot-terrorists/.

WORKING WHILE AUTISTIC

KELLY BRON JOHNSON

I started working when I was thirteen, but the hustle was in me much before that. Anything I could sell, I would. I made bracelets and sold them. I had a special interest in entomology, so I even collected and sold slugs (I made one sale!). I babysat, I worked in fast food, I worked at the SPCA, in offices—you name it, I've probably done it.

I've currently settled on being an online content creator and digital marketer. This means I write web content for the company I work for, and take care of their Search Engine Optimisation (SEO), Search Engine Marketing (SEM), and social media management. Though I was working full-time in an office for a year and a half and mostly happy, I recently changed jobs to a position where I am able to work from home. This hasn't been without its own set of hiccoughs, which I will delve into a bit further on.

From an early age, my mother walked me through all the etiquette for getting jobs and looking professional. She taught me how to address people on the phone, how to write a cover letter, how to act, and what to say during an interview. I still to this day send thank-you notes after an interview. It might be considered old-fashioned, but it works. I think the reason it's easy for me to get a job is because I could memorize the social rules and script. It's a persona I can put on and perform. Politeness and professionalism go such a long way and there are simple rules: show up on time. Dress properly and neatly. Shake hands, make eye contact. Smile. Say "please" and "thank you." The "performance" lasts an hour or less. For that time, I can blend in and look "normal." No one would guess I'm autistic. That said, those are the rules to getting a job. Those are not the rules to keeping a job.

I was once told by a boss I had no ego. Whatever I was asked to do, I did, without complaint. I've mopped floors, cleaned dog poop, and washed out oil vats. I wore crappy-looking uniforms. I went to university classes smelling like fries. I spent a summer almost never seeing the light of day while stuck in a basement making photocopies for lawyers. The point is, I've always been able to get a job—doesn't mean it was a good one!—and I've pretty much always had a job of some sort. I've even worked four jobs at once.

These are examples, however, of how we can sometimes be taken advantage of. Our loyalty and strong work ethic, combined with not always being able to read people, mean that we can end up in situations where we get saddled with more than our fair share and are overworked and underpaid.

I have a hard time saying no to work. Even when I have a full time job, I still tend to want to take on more, or take a class or freelance contract. I think I get excited about the novelty of doing something new or different and then I overcommit.

Overcommitting, however, has led to a lot of feelings of panic and overwhelm. When I have too much on my plate, my brain goes into overdrive and executive function (I call it executive dysfunction) issues start to rear their ugly head. I become overwhelmed by everything I have to do, and then freeze and can get nothing done at all. I no longer know where to start or even how to start. I then become angry at myself and fear letting everyone down. Because of this, I have had bosses tell me I'm an inconsistent performer, and it's true.

Either I overdeliver because I'm hyper-focused and in my stride, or I do the bare minimum because I'm overwhelmed. The trick has been trying to find a place where I can always perform at my best and not be distracted or side-tracked.

Hyperfocus can also cause problems of its own. It isn't a bad thing when I want to get work done, but it can mean I forget to go to the bathroom, leave the office, or eat. There were many times I did not realize the work day was over until I suddenly noticed everyone else had left the office. Because of this, I have learned to set timers on my phone, or calendar reminders to eat lunch and to go home. There are times I have set alarms to remind me to breathe because I realized I was breathing very shallowly and it was causing a lot of tension in my body. I have to check in with my body frequently and make a note to breathe deeply, and relax any tension in my shoulders or elsewhere. I also have to sometimes actually remind myself to change position or just move.

The physical environment at work can also be challenging for me, namely things I cannot control within it. I have sensory issues with strong perfumes. I'm not a fan of bright lights, much preferring to work in natural light or the dark. I can deal with office noise and chatter, but cannot tolerate whispers. I also very much dislike alarms or repetitive beeping. I hear cell phone chimes, people clicking pens, people tapping, people chewing, people breathing too loudly—I hear it all and can be distracted. Sometimes I work with headphones on, either without music or with white noise or ocean waves (my favourite nature sound).

I also have problems with temperature. It seems most offices are either too hot or freezing, or fluctuate wildly throughout the day. In particular, I don't seem to register when I'm starting to get too hot. For example, if the day started off cool, I might drape a sweater over my shoulders. Once the office starts to warm up, I don't seem to take mental note of it. Instead, I start to sweat heavily, and then my body starts to panic. Only when my heart starts beating quickly do I realize I am sweating—and only then will I think to take off the sweater. By then, I am dizzy and in full panic attack mode. Because it creeps up on me, for the longest time, I did not realize I was having a panic attack simply due to the temperature changing. I almost rely on other people to say, "Hey, it's getting hot. Are you hot?" before I can take a mental note of it and check in with my body.

Before I got diagnosed, I didn't understand that I was coming across to others as rude, abrupt, standoffish, and a know-it-all. I essentially did not have a tactful or diplomatic bone in my body and that's something I'm still trying to smooth over.

I was also too naive to play office politics, and I was easily manipulated. Because of my strong sense of justice and honesty, and because of essentially having no fear to say it like it is, people used me as their voice for complaints. So I was the one telling the boss about everyone else's problems, but I was the one who looked bad as a result. I looked like a complainer or tattle-taler.

I'm also highly intelligent—not saying that to boast, but it's a fact, I've had my IQ tested—and that can be very intimidating for others, even when it unintentionally comes out. It took me a long time before I realized people don't like to be corrected, and people don't like to lose face. Simply feeling compelled to get the facts right for the record did not win me any friends, even though I didn't think I was being rude or felt it was anything personal against them. I've learnt a lot of it comes down to me keeping my mouth shut. Not everything in my head needs to be declared out loud, and I'd rather be seen as quiet than rude. I now resist the urge to jump into other people's conversations, even though I feel like I have a lot of interesting things to contribute. I've also modeled the behaviour and language of more diplomatic people, and I continue to develop my skills at diplomacy.

Because I have self-doubt issues, I need a lot of feedback from others to let me know I'm on the right track. I also have auditory processing issues, and if you give me a series of commands or directions verbally, I will hear it and think I got it all, only to sit down at my desk and remember nothing. If I go back and ask for a repeat, I can be seen as unintelligent or incompetent, so after my diagnosis, I was able to realize I simply need to have directions written down. It's not because I'm unintelligent; I simply process things differently. I now ask to have either my boss write it down (or email me) or allow me to take the notes I need.

Although I am working from home now and there is less office drama for me to worry about, I sometimes still have problems communicating. With my new job, I wanted to express to my boss that I was uncomfortable with her management style and the way bits of work were being thrown at me and changed unexpectedly. I thought I was being clear in how I expressed myself, but it turns out I wasn't. So I let it bottle up in me until I wanted to quit. When it finally came out, it was a shock to her. To her great credit, we opened up the dialogue so we could both be understood and are giving it another try. I'm thirty-six and it's the first time I was able to stick it out to learn how to communicate better, instead of running in fear that no one will understand me.

I believe communication is a two-way street and I do have to compromise somewhat. My boss is more extroverted and craves face-to-face contact and collaboration. We've decided to meet one day a week in the office. I've discovered that even if I don't necessarily read people's body language very well, for some people's comfort, they need to read mine. Even if they get it wrong because I don't always give off the correct "vibes," for some people, they need to see my body language.

Our office uses webcams for some meetings, and because I can see myself on the screen, I've discovered I look a lot more serious than I feel. My face just cannot work itself into the expressions I'm feeling. Not without what feels to me like a lot of exaggeration. When I think I'm smiling, it barely registers in the camera pointing back at me. I am realizing for the first time that my facial expressions—or lack of facial expressions—misrepresent my actual emotions and how I want to be perceived. I thought I looked a lot happier, but I don't, not without conscious effort.

Another major difficulty I had, more so in my twenties than now, was simply being flighty. I've met a few other autistic females like me. One I know, in addition to changing jobs, would also pick up and move to a different city or apartment. Like me, she can be restless and loves to travel. We're a particular breed of autistic. We're flighty, indecisive at times, but we dream big (or maybe naively) and take risks. We feel the need to get away, maybe to avoid—but while we don't do well with outside change, when we control the change, we can do it. We'll redecorate a room, book a flight out of the country, or go on a road trip. It comes from a mix of great restlessness, needing novelty, and not wanting to deal with reality. Because of this, when a work situation became challenging—either I was bored or wasn't getting along with someone—I used to find it easier to just quit and find another job. Although finding a job wasn't my problem, finding a good job and keeping it was. Not because I got fired—I never have been—but because I always wanted to make sure I quit before I was fired.

Sometimes I've gotten down on myself for being a quitter. Maybe I could have found a way to confront and fix my problems rather than run, or maybe there was a lesson I was missing. Perhaps, I thought, I was just flawed and broken, so no one could ever like me. I'd even convinced myself I simply couldn't work a regular 9-5 job. I told myself there were too many rules in an office to follow, too much authority. I told myself I was incapable, and that was my real failing. This led to a lot of self-confidence issues and depression.

The plus side to being quick to leave a situation is that it is a valid survivor instinct and a good one, when the situation is actually abusive. However, I believe I took the tendency to leave too far, too quickly. So while I did have enough awareness to protect myself, the choices I had to make were not always the best. I've gone into debt to make sure I pay bills and being in a precarious financial situation is stressful.

Luckily, I had a husband to support me during times I quit and had no income, so I never starved or had to worry about being homeless. But I was unpredictable. I could easily call him any given afternoon and tell him I quit yet another job, and that I had booked myself a solo trip to Morocco, leaving next week, using my last paycheck. It put a lot of stress on our relationship.

I've become better at recognizing when I really do need to quit a job. Signs for me that I am in the wrong job include having frequent panic attacks, lacking motivation, or being bored. Because of the flighty or restless part of my personality, if I don't have the right amount of mental stimulation at my job, I need extra work or I become bored and do nothing. I can also have a panic attack from being bored because my brain needs constant stimulation. If there is no external stimulation, it creates its own excitement in the form of a panic attack. Also, if I leave work feeling totally drained, I know I've spent too much energy fighting the demons of sensory overload.

My recent job change wasn't because I was particularly unhappy at my previous job; I liked and got along well with my co-workers and they were very accommodating and understanding. But I was leaving work tired after an eight-hour day under fluorescent lighting and fluctuating temperatures. The most productive time for me was when everyone left the office—the lights would go out and it was quiet. Unfortunately, I had the whole day to get through and account for. So while I was dealing with it and wasn't looking for a new job, when an opportunity came up for me to work from home, I jumped at it and it has been amazing for me. I now have my home office set up as I like. I am in control of my environment. I sit on a balance ball as my office chair. I have fidgets and tangles to keep my hands busy when I want, without having to worry about anyone looking at me strangely. There's no one whispering, or wearing strong perfumes, or tapping pens annoyingly. As a result, I feel more relaxed and have more energy at the end of my day.

Because I didn't get diagnosed until I was thirty-two, any problems I had, I didn't understand what they were. I kept fighting through them. I kept blaming myself. I couldn't understand why I had such a hard time just being like everyone else. I didn't understand why I seemed to struggle more or why I couldn't get along with people, even when I thought I was being a good friend. When something wasn't a good fit, I saw no problem quitting and looking for something else. I didn't realize that I was not coping because of how I processed the world. I didn't realize I was experiencing sensory overload on a daily basis.

It wasn't until my first son was diagnosed as autistic that I sought diagnosis for myself. I saw way too many similarities in our childhoods. At first, I wasn't self-aware enough to really see it in myself, but then I started reading books by other autistic females and completely related to them. I then opted for formal diagnosis and got it.

I think what prompted me to really accept myself and learn self-advocacy was finding my "tribe"—other autistic adults. Through online communities, I have connected with people who are just like me, with the same struggles and quirks, and we get along really well. Through them, I learned how to advocate for myself, and that I can and should advocate for myself, following their examples. I consider some of these people my real friends now, even though many of us haven't met in real life. We just understand each other and watch out for each other. It's a world of acceptance I never had until I found them.

All my pre-diagnosis work experiences were not wasted, however. I gained a lot of experience doing different types of jobs. I was taken out of my comfort zone and learned new skills. I was able to learn my strengths and weaknesses and started to understand what a good place to work was for me. Over time, I stopped taking just any job and started to be more choosey for myself. I've also learned what is worth tolerating and sacrificing oneself for and what is not. I've become less restless and flighty. I think all that comes with confidence and maturity over time.

Now I believe not all my difficulties can be fixed, or at least not without being met halfway, but it can be better. I disclose my diagnosis now in interviews because I've decided that if it's going to be enough of an issue for them not to hire me, I would rather not even try to work there. The best places to work are those that have a curious attitude. After I disclose, if they say, "ok, you're autistic. What do we need to know? What do we need to do?" then I know we're on the right track. Then we can talk about accommodations. We can talk about communication, or how I prefer to organize my day, my tasks, and my work. Then we can see if it's a good fit. I tell them I can't tolerate strong scents and that I need to have directions written down. I explain I have strengths as well, because of my autism, like my focus, creativity, and ease at spotting errors.

I also don't hide my autism in my online presence—my LinkedIn profile has a post I made about seeking work accommodations, as well as my position as an autistic board member for a Canadian national nonprofit organization. Any employer who Googles my name or looks at my profile will see these facts about me. So if they do their research, they will know before even calling me in for an interview.

Post-diagnosis, I know more about myself and how I can set myself up to succeed. I have the ability and confidence to advocate for myself. I am not jumping from one place to another as quickly or often. I am much more comfortable being able to be myself at work. I'm not having daily panic attacks due to sensory issues. I can be much more productive and happy.

I am still a work in progress and still learning more methods to cope with my sensory issues and executive function. I am open to tools and technology or whatever is needed to help me work with my brain. I now accept my brain how it is, and it has a lot of pluses despite some of the struggles. I see a therapist so I can be as effective as possible as a person, and as comfortable in my own body as I can possibly be. In therapy, we're working on my self-esteem, depression and complex post-traumatic stress disorder from childhood trauma. Not understanding or accepting myself was a big source of trouble, but not having parents to love and accept me as I am was the most damaging. I'm still very guarded and slow to trust people, but as scary as it is, I keep trying and putting myself out there because that's the only way to grow.

The best advice I can give comes only with time and practice: have the confidence to be yourself and let others learn who you are. Learn about yourself and what works and doesn't work for you. But also take a few chances and try some new things because you will still learn something from the experience no matter what. It is okay to accept the good and the bad about yourself. It is okay to accept that there are times you will easily feel at your limit in certain situations and others where you can go further. Don't let fear stop you from trying. Just accept that things are different for you and try to work with yourself rather than against yourself.

ABOUT THE AUTHOR

Kelly Bron Johnson got her autism diagnosis only as an adult, in her thirties. Diagnosis gave her answers, helped her find her tribe, and gave her the confidence to launch into self-advocacy. She serves on the board of a Canadian national nonprofit organization and is a disability accessibility consultant through her business, Completely Inclusive. She works full time in Digital Marketing and lives in Montreal, Canada with her husband and two sons. You can keep up to date with her via linktr.ee/kbronjohn.

ALL OF ME: HOW DO I KNOW WHERE BLACKNESS ENDS AND NEURODIVERGENCE BE-GINS?

Morénike Giwa Onaiwu

I am an autistic adult who was diagnosed in my thirties, just a few years ago. I am also a parent (of both autistic and non-autistic children). I am also black. And a woman. And an educator. An advocate. An American with immigrant parents. A Christian. An adoptive parent. A person with ADHD. A writer (at least an aspiring one). And more. There are so many different aspects of my identity...you could say that I am "intersectionality" personified. And it would be true. But it is probably true for you as well.

Most of us have multiple identities. Few (actually, probably no) people in this world can claim a existence that's purely homogeneous. We are all unique in some way, and usually in several ways. However, there's a pretty distinct difference in our perspectives and our experiences when our specific differences fall within marginalized and/or minority groups rather than within groups with more privilege. And even though we are all still humans and by virtue of that we have a lot of similarities with other humans, this still makes for a monumental difference—about as different as Venus is from Earth.

When the differences have to do with race, gender, disability, and/or culture, etc., you often find yourself trying to determine "which" aspect of your personhood is at play in a particular situation. It's very challenging, and very draining. And at best, it's an educated guess. Because you never really know.

Whether x is good or x is bad, you have to wonder if x is all that it appears to be. Or perhaps at least partially did x happen the way it did because I'm female presenting? Or because I'm black? Because I'm black AND female presenting? Or maybe none of those, but it was more due to autistic mannerisms? Or perhaps it was a cultural thing instead, something that would have made sense to "real" Americans—not new ones like myself and my family? Or maybe I'm misreading all of it and it was really more of a conservative Christian thing and that's why I'm lost, since I'm not a conservative?

And that's just one hour of the day...

And that's just me, not including situations involving my kids, who have numerous intersectionalities of their own.

Maybe you have similar questions. Maybe you replay scenarios in your mind that have occurred and wonder if they would have had the same outcomes if you weren't...well, you. If you were neurotypical, would something in your life have unfolded in a completely different way? Or if you were noticeably gender non-conforming as well as autistic? If you were a different age? A different cultural or religious background?

I wonder these types of things all the time. In this piece, I will let you wander—and wonder—along with me about this thing that I still haven't figured out in thirty-something years of being me. Accompany me on a few events on a hypothetical week. (And, BTW, all of the things I mention here have actually happened in some way or another, to me. Not all in the same week, but they're still true events. In other words, this piece is "based on a true story.")

You ready? Let's roll.

ॐ

It's Sunday. We go to a restaurant after church. We order our food. We modify the meals to accommodate food allergies, food preferences and aversions, and sensory needs, but we do so politely.

My kids are boisterous at the table, joking with one another and chatting, the teens occasionally bickering over nonsense. My youngest daughter gleefully recites a few verbal scripts while my youngest son stims vocally with his current sound. It's kind of a cross between a song, a whistle, and a muted shriek. But we aren't any louder in volume or more disruptive in our actions than any other family in the restaurant, though our sounds might differ from theirs.

Our server is not openly rude, but pretty disengaged and inattentive—when we can find them. They scarcely return to refill water or to check to see if we need anything, though we see them attending dutifully to other tables. It's clear to me that the server assumes that we're not going to tip, so there's no need to pay attention to us. However, they are dead wrong. I was raised right. I certainly don't plan to give a ginormous tip in this instance because the service we've received doesn't warrant that, but I still leave my minimum 20% tip. When I sign my receipt indicating the tip, the server's surprise—and subsequent remorse at ignoring us—is apparent.

Why are they surprised? Why were they so dismissive of us and inattentive?

Maybe it's because I'm black and they subscribe to the "black people don't tip" stereotype.

Maybe it's because even though I mentioned my kids were autistic, they didn't trash the eating area and leave it looking like a war zone.

Maybe it's because when I mentioned the food modifications I referenced autism, etc., and they assumed we'd be a pain to deal with (because apparently autistic people are stereotyped as "difficult").

Maybe it's because since my husband was at work they perceived me as a single mother.

Maybe I'll never know exactly why.

It's Monday. I'm running afternoon errands with my kids in tow (as usual). We are standing in a lobby waiting for an elevator, and while we wait my daughter is reading the signs posted on the walls aloud, which are at adult level and fairly complex. A woman who was also waiting remarked, "You must come here a lot to have memorized all of these signs." When my daughter replied that she'd never been in this building before, the woman was astonished. "But you're just a little girl. Surely you're not reading all of that?" she asked. "Yes," my daughter answered matter of factly, "I've been reading since I was two years old." She then began to read the summary on the back of the novel that the woman was holding aloud (it was at my daughter's eye level).

The woman's surprise—do I attribute it mainly due to a disability-related factor, namely my daughter's hyperlexia as a twice exceptional child (gifted and autistic)? Did the fact that my daughter is a black child with such abilities also contribute to her surprise?

It's Tuesday. I'm at work in my classroom, teaching. Midway through the period one of my colleagues knocks on my door and then pops a head in the doorway, apologetically asking if I can keep it just a little quieter since their class next door can hear my voice. I agree, apologizing as well. It is difficult for me after that to get my mind back in gear for a few moments. To compensate for unknowingly being too loud, I intentionally begin to speak more softly, but now my students complain that they can't understand me clearly. I couldn't seem to find that "just right" tone that was in between loud and quiet. It was frustrating.

This has happened before, and just like the previous times I hadn't at all realized that I was loud. To my own ears, my volume wasn't loud at all, just normal. How, I wondered yet again, would I be able to succeed in speaking more quietly if I couldn't recognize when I was being loud in the first place?

One characteristic that I share with other autistics is differences in social communication. It varies by circumstance, but essentially our pragmatics, prosody, vocabulary, etc., tend to differ from that of others. Was this inability to regulate my tone an autistic thing? Along with some of my other communication differences?

Maybe you're like me, and as long as you can remember the way you spoke was never really like everybody else...maybe you too were viewed as a "little professor" because of the way you talked. Maybe you also hate (and suck at) small talk. Maybe you struggled to know what to say and how to say it in conversations. Maybe you spoke late or didn't speak much at all. Maybe you repeated things (echolalia), and/or used a lot of scripted phrases and song lyrics (like I still do). Maybe when you are passionate about something you can talk about it nonstop and not realize that the other person isn't really responding back.

And on top of that, maybe your tone of voice is never really what others consider "normal." For me, my volume was always perceived to be either way too loud or way too quiet. Both in the classroom and in other settings.

But then I thought of my parents, and my uncles, and aunts. The loud, animated conversations that they have in person and/or via telephone are almost always pretty high volume, and have been as long as I can remember—and they're not all autistic (most of them aren't autistic at all). Furthermore, I've noticed this among other people of color (PoC) too outside of my own family. Maybe some of this loudness is just a PoC thing? Or maybe it's both an autistic and a PoC thing? How can I tell?

It's Wednesday. Worship music blares through the speakers. The bass ripples through my body. The drumbeat invigorates me. I move. I move. I am one with the music as I dance before God. I don't know the words of the song and I don't need to because my heart is singing. I sway with my arms raised, then with my arms at my sides, my head bopping to the rhythm. I worship wholly, and freely, and happily.

The song ends and another starts. The music is loud, but in a pleasant way. I almost don't hear the muffled "Excuse me." But then I hear it a second time as it is accompanied by a tap on my shoulder. I turn around.

A woman seated in the row behind me glances sheepishly at me and gestures to a Kleenex box in my row a few seats away from me. Her right hand is cupped over her nose. I understand now why she sounded muffled and what she is hiding beneath her hand; after all, it's allergy season. I hand her the box, and she replies with a muffled, "Thank you," and a grateful smile that is half-hidden by her hand. I smile back.

As I start to turn back around I feel someone's gaze on me. I look back again and notice that there is a man sitting next to her, presumably her man from their body language/close proximity. While the woman is preoccupied with attempting to clean her nostrils discreetly, he makes eye contact with me. He smiles at me. I don't like his smile—it unnerves me. I don't smile back. He proceeds to give me a once-over, eyes lingering hungrily on certain parts of my anatomy. Creep. I feel suddenly uncomfortable and turn back around.

The music is still booming. But the joy has vanished from it. I play the last several minutes back in my head and see myself dancing. Only now rather than perceiving it from the perspective of someone worshiping, I take a more carnal approach. I imagine someone leering at my hips gyrating, my buttocks jiggling, my breasts bouncing as I praise the Lord the only way I know how—fully and truly. Innocently. I am a black woman and this is the body God gave me. It has curves. That's not a crime.

I am an autistic Christian. I don't do put-on pleasantries. I don't go through the motions. Everything I do is raw and real. My faith is new to me, something I only acquired in adulthood. I don't have rituals and tradition to fall back on. I only have my sincere faith, and an innocent desire to praise God totally with all that I am. Mind, body, and soul. Only at this moment the "body" part was being corrupted by fear and doubt due to the actions of another.

I felt no shame in my movements because there was nothing wrong with me dancing, but now I was worried. Was this man—who, from what I could tell, obviously had a wandering eye—going to get the wrong idea? Had he already gotten the wrong idea that I was trying to flirt or turn him on somehow by the way I dance? Would his woman get upset at me if he kept looking at me, maybe thinking I was trying to make a pass at her man (because, again, I am a black woman after all, so I am potentially "loose" and devoid of morals, right)? And because I am autistic, it isn't likely that I would handle either scenario (him choosing to misread my signals or her misconstruing the situation) well. Sigh. I didn't want nor need any drama.

I sat woodenly in my chair. I wanted to worship as I had been doing earlier. But I felt trapped by my need to self-protect. I knew the dangers of not catching these kinds of signs and being in an unpleasant situation as a result. I've been in that place before. I didn't want it today. Not here, in the house of God. And not now when I had enough going on in my life.

I got up and moved to another seat far away from his undressing eyes. But the damage was already done. Even here, in my new seat, I couldn't relax. The peace and joy that I had at the beginning of the service was long gone. I couldn't wait for it to end so I could just go home.

Maybe you've also been in situations where you felt shamed for the way you naturally move. Perhaps you too have experienced situations where someone misread your body movements as something they were not, such as flirtation, or aggression. Maybe you have felt forced to "tone down" your movements because of the potential reactions of others, whether your movements are dancing, flapping, spinning, toe walking, or not making eye contact. Maybe you too have found that you can't even be safe inside of your own body.

It's Thursday. I am looking for some document that I can't find and that of course I really need. I shuffle through stacks of paperwork that I have in my desk, on my desk, in my drawers (where clothing should be), in plastic bags, on shelves. I look and look and look. I find all types of things. Much of it I don't need. Some of it is very important.

I come across some of my youngest daughter's old evaluations. Before we knew she was autistic she was still "receiving services" for other things, including speech and OT. I skimmed through the stack of pages. On paper, my daughter was a living, breathing list of deficits. Page after page about what she couldn't do, didn't do, or didn't do enough of.

In one particular assessment report, my eyes rested on one paragraph. I could practically quote it. In it, the "professional" was making their case for why they believed my daughter was likely intellectually disabled, citing her echolalia and lack of "original, spontaneous speech" as supporting reasons. Even though her intellect had not yet been formally assessed, they were already making presumptions about her abilities as if speech and intellect are intertwined.

It comes as no surprise to me that autistic children of color are more likely to be identified as intellectually disabled than their white counterparts; the same is true of children of color who are not autistic. This concerns me. Not because being diagnosed with an intellectual disability is the worst thing in the world; it is not. But because of the disproportionality in the diagnosis. Children of color, as well as nonspeaking individuals, are quick to be identified as "deficient" or "lacking" in some way, but their strengths and abilities are not as readily determined. Why?

Why?

It turned out that this esteemed "professional" was completely and totally wrong about my child's cognitive ability; my daughter had IQ testing conducted approximately a year after that report and that is when we discovered that she was gifted. And though I would have loved her exactly the same regardless of IQ, it is unclear to me which characteristic was the driving factor behind an assumption by "professionals" of intellectual impairment in the absence of evidence or formal testing. They had written her off without even verifying if their hypothesis was right or wrong. How much of a role did disability play in their presumptions; how much of a role did race play? Had she been a young white girl with the same profile would the same assumption have been reached? Or if she still was a black girl, but one without a disability, would they have reserved judgment?

Maybe you were also disregarded by "professionals" when you were in school—or even now. Maybe you found that there was a lot of emphasis on what you couldn't do and little attention paid to your strengths—like my daughter. Or maybe it was the opposite for you (like it was for me), and it seemed to some that your abilities overshadowed your support needs...maybe you didn't get the help you deserved because everyone felt that you were "smart enough" to be able to "figure it out on your own."

It's Friday. School is out and my teens want to hit the mall. I am tired and the last place that I feel like going is the mall. But when I ponder it a bit I recall that Friday nights at the mall are much more calm than Saturday afternoons. On Saturdays the mall is like a zoo. Too many people; too many smells; too many sounds. Yuck. I gathered my spoons, loaded my kids in the car, and headed for the mall.

After stopping in a gazillion smaller shops, we eventually end up in one of the large, high end department stores. The teens are starting to get into brand names a bit, and were looking at some of the clothes. They looked at several clothing combinations from different parts of the store, and opted to try a few of them on.

One of my sons, the oldest one, was looking for a particular clothing item. We looked, but couldn't find it. Walking a little ahead of us, my son approached a salesperson to ask for help.

I watched the exchange from where I was standing not far away. It seemed as though the salesperson was having trouble understanding my son. My son doesn't always make eye contact when speaking to others, and sometimes there are lengthy pauses in his speech as he mentally searches for the right word. There may also be a pause before he actually begins to speak while he processes what has been said to him.

This doesn't mean that he cannot be understood. He can. But sometimes it requires that someone exercise a little patience in order for them to converse.

The salesperson's facial expression indicated that he was a little confused by what my son was saying. My son tried repeating himself, but I guess it still wasn't coming out right. I saw him lift his head and start scanning the room for me. I met my son's gaze, and he beckoned for me to come over.

I walked over to where they were, and tried to clarify what my son was saying. As soon as I joined them, the salesperson's whole demeanor changed. He (the salesperson) noticeably relaxed in my presence. While I was speaking, he nodded and smiled. I wasn't sure what I had done that was so special, but I was glad that seemingly we were getting somewhere.

So I thought, anyway. When I finished talking, the salesperson turned to my son and began addressing him.

Whereas before I had come over the salesperson was speaking to my son "normally," now he was engaging in what I call "baby talk." You know the loud, higher-pitched, exaggerated manner a lot of adults use to communicate with babies? Many people also speak that same way to disabled people. Apparently my coming over alerted the salesperson that my son was Not a Regular Person. The presence of a parent (or, as some people say, a paaaaaaaaarent) signified to the salesperson that something must be wrong with my son because he needed my support. Therefore, somehow even though he and my son were speaking to one another normally just minutes prior, now my son needed to be spoken to in babyspeak. Because disabled people are just babies in adult bodies. Right?

I felt myself getting annoyed and considered calling attention to the nonsense. But then I felt a little conflicted. You see, my son, who is, like me, black, is 14 years old and taller than me. His voice has changed and he sounds more like a young man than a boy. He still, to me, looks like a kid rather than an adult. But we live in a world where police can gun down twelve-year-old old black males with toy weapons in the street with impunity and where officers can shoot at an unarmed man of color in the street for brandishing a toy truck;

what looks like a growing teen who is obviously still childlike to my eyes may be viewed as a menacing threat to someone else. And this salesperson hadn't treated my son as if he was scared of his blackness.

The baby talk was humiliating. I pictured my son squirming on the inside. He's a nice kid, so he wouldn't say anything directly to the man. But I knew he was bothered by it—because I was. At least I suspected he was bothered by it.

Part of me said, "Say something! You're his mom! His protector! Don't let someone unknowingly disrespect him like this!"

But the other part of me said, "The man is being ableist. But he isn't being racist. Shouldn't I be grateful? He didn't follow my son around the store, or falsely accuse him of shoplifting, or treat him with disdain for being black. He is treating him with disdain for being disabled, not for being black. This is humiliating, yes. But humiliation isn't as likely to kill you as racism is. Maybe I should leave well enough alone..."

Maybe you too have been forced to choose life over dignity. One ism over the other.

The tug of war. The date changes. The players change. The scenario changes. The struggle doesn't. It doesn't.

Which one will I fight for and which one will I sacrifice?

It's Saturday. It's been a long week.

I watch the news.

Or I go online.

Or I hear it from someone.

It hits me like a punch to the stomach. It hurts.

Another person like me. Dead.

Dead. Maybe they're disabled. Maybe they're a person of color. Maybe they're a woman. Maybe they're a combination of some or all of those characteristics. Whatever the case, they are no longer living.

Maybe they were killed by a parent, caregiver, or spouse who "snapped" due to the "burden" of caring for a disabled family member.

Or maybe they were killed because they were in the wrong place at the wrong time while black. Another hashtag that won't get justice.

Or maybe they killed themselves. Because they internalized the messages of self-hatred and worthlessness that society fed them about who they are. They couldn't bear the thought of living their lives any longer. They ended things.

Maybe they overdosed. Many substance users are self-medicating to cope with their present and bury their past. The rate of substance use, mental health diagnoses, etc., is high among both individuals with disabilities and people of color. It is also high among women.

Maybe they died of malnutrition or preventable illness. Access to quality care and services fluctuates widely, with some groups having more than others. These disparities fuel poorer health outcomes, lower quality of life, and higher morbidity rates among marginalized groups. Not surprisingly, the disabled, women, and people of color are high on that list in terms of risk factors.

Different days. Different names. Different situations.

Same need.

I—and people like me—can't splinter ourselves. There is no disabled me. There is no black me. There is no female me. There is no parent me. There is no Christian me. There is just...me. All of me. And I need for all of me—all these parts of me—to be addressed. I can't leave my leg out in the rain while the rest of my body comes indoors for shelter. Because if I do I am still going to be wet and miserable, even if much of my body is dry. That won't work for me.

I don't know where my blackness stops and my femaleness begins. I don't know where my femaleness stops and my Christianity begins. I don't know where my role as a disabled adult stops and where my role as a parent begins. I don't know when my role as a parent stops and my autisticness begins. I don't know where my autisticness stops and my blackness begins. And rinse, no-poo, repeat.

I didn't stop being black when I found out I was autistic. I didn't stop being a woman when I found out I was autistic. I didn't stop being me. Everything that affected how I live, how I think, how I feel, who I am—still applies. I am not immune to the issues related to race, gender, or other aspects of my identity because I am autistic. My autistic identity is added to that equation; it removed nothing from it.

And because so many years of my life passed before I had a full understanding of these things, it's even more critical to me that solutions, policies, ideas, images, writing, research, HAVE to be intersectional. I need them to address all of me. All of me. No longer will I splinter myself for others' comfort or for any well-intended but incomplete cause.

All of me. Or none of me. I want it all.

Or nothing at all.

ABOUT THE AUTHOR

Morénike Giwa Onaiwu is a global community advocate, writer and educator who is passionate about human rights, justice, and inclusion. Her undergraduate and graduate degrees are in International Relations and Education. She is the proud mother of six beautiful biological and adoptive children; together they comprise a proud multicultural, multinational, neurodiverse, HIV affected family of color. She blogs about her life at Who Needs Normalcy (http://whoneeds-normalcy.blogspot.com/).

USING INTERSECTING IDENTITIES AND RADICALLY ACCEPTING COMMUNITIES TO INCREASE COPING SKILLS

Samantha Hack

Autistic people do best when raised in an accommodating environment and allowed to choose from a variety of coping mechanisms and techniques, learn from other autistics, and live our lives as we see fit. If we are lucky, the only boundaries we face are those we impose on ourselves. That happens occasionally—certainly more often now than in the past, due to the neurodiversity movement's focus on shifting simple awareness of autism toward active acceptance of autistic people.

However, many autistic people like me still go undiagnosed well into adulthood, and have no accommodations for large swaths of our lives. We are left to scrounge for coping techniques, compiling a patchwork of tools for disparate diagnoses. These tools sometimes enable the surface appearance of neurotypicality. This is a veneer imposed by society, and one that in my case was far from healthy.

When I discovered I was autistic, it was, without hyperbole, the greatest revelation of my life.

Getting to that point was not easy. I am in my late thirties and only just now learning what it means to be autistic. Between misconceptions, internalized hatred and ableism, and a history of depression and growing anxiety, I often wonder how it is I managed to make it this far on my own.

When I look back at my life through the lens of autism, I can see that my trial by fire, my sink-or-swim exposure to society at large, left me with more coping skills than I had realized. My hard-learned lessons were the basis of the very coping techniques that allowed me to survive.

While some autistics grow up with accommodations that help them learn autism-specific coping techniques and skills, I learned to adapt coping techniques and skills from mainstream sources. At the time I was completely unaware that I was doing this to meet autism-related needs; I can only see that looking back on it now.

If there is one thing I would call "good" about being diagnosed late in life, it is that I learned how to take coping skills from one area of my life and apply them to other areas. I did this out of necessity, and don't think I would have done it if I had been diagnosed early.

That is not to say that going undiagnosed for so long was a blessing. It was not, at least not for me. Living undiagnosed for so long meant a rollercoaster ride of functionality and dysfunctionality, with wild swings between flawless self-sufficiency and massive executive dysfunction. When I had complete control of my life and my environment, I did well. When I did not, I floundered, and was left wondering what was wrong with me. I had no way to explain why I could not meet others' expectations.

It would be easy to say that because I managed, anyone could, but that isn't true—and if I were offered the opportunity to go back and relive my childhood, I would only do so if I could have a formal diagnosis, effective accommodations, and support. The people I've known who've grown up with that have coping tools that are infinitely more varied and usable than what I could learn on my own.

Despite having to develop coping skills without proper support, I learned a lot, and what I have learned is extremely valuable. As I progress through therapy I find myself regularly telling my therapist, "I already do that for..." on a regular basis. And now that I know I am autistic, acquiring new coping skills is even easier.

Identifying, Isolating, and Transferring Scripts and Skills

While growing up, I learned many scripts for social interactions that were ultimately harmful. As I replace those with new, healthier versions, I find myself naturally reaching out to my intersecting identities. For example, I am transfeminine, physically disabled, and have OCD, and have scripts and skills to help with each of these—and those can help with being autistic. Likewise, scripts and skills I use for autism can help me cope in other areas.

To use a skill I initially developed for something else, I first identify and isolate the skill. When I identify a coping skill, I am figuring out, broadly, what I'm doing that is helpful. When I isolate a skill, I'm distilling the skill to its most basic essence. If I am going to take a skill from one context and use it in a different context, I need to be able to do so with as little (and preferably no) pollution from the initial context.

I have a little stuffed fox that I carry around with in my backpack at school. When I am experiencing a sensory overload in class, I will play with the fox by rubbing its ears. Identifying this skill means recognizing it as stimming for sensory regulation. When I isolate that skill I am asking, "What specific benefits am I getting, and what precisely am I doing that causes those benefits?" The answer is that because I am tactilely oriented (hypersensitive to touch), stroking something soft directs my attention to my immediate environment, allowing me to focus instead of having my attention drift around the classroom. It is the softness that specifically matters, and having isolated that, I have a new skill to acquire for use in other contexts. I don't need that specific toy; I can use anything soft, including patches on my purse, the sleeves on my sweater, or anything, really.

I can also transfer that skill to use for other issues. Wearing soft-sleeved sweaters helps me manage my tactile hypersensitivity and my OCD by providing pleasant sensations on my arms that are more noticeable than other sensations. Since I know that soft things focus my attention, when I have an anxiety attack, I can find anything soft, rub it between my fingers, and use that to focus on the cognitive-behavioral therapy techniques I use to redirect my thoughts.

Identifying a skill allows me to figure out the basics of a coping technique, but it is isolating skills—reducing them to their most basic essences—that lets me get the most out of a particular skill and maximize the number of ways it can be used in other contexts.

This ability to identify, isolate, and transfer skills is a coping technique in and of itself. It is this primary coping skill that drives my self-exploration and allows me to walk the line between being unapologetically, openly autistic and passing as neurotypical.

Transition Skills as Coping Tools for Emotional Regulation

I spent the vast majority of my life trying to pass as a man. Though it was the gender I was assigned at birth, I found the concepts of manliness and masculinity to be daunting, overwhelming, and utterly confusing. It is safe to say that by society's standards I was not a very good man.

It took me thirty-three years to figure that out. When I did, I jumped into the deep end of the gender pool and did not look back. I started shedding what little male socialization I had and deliberately focused on the female socialization that I naturally picked up throughout my life.

A lot of female socialization came to me naturally. The way I walk, I was told, is very feminine. The way I sit, as well. When I speak, I speak with typically feminine inflections and patterns. I had been ridiculed for these ways of moving and speaking all my life because society saw me as the wrong gender, and now they help define who I am.

When I was perceived as a man I was often treated as an average man even when I did not understand social cues or my social standing. That treatment was imposed on me by others whether I wanted it or not. I was able to be dominant in conversation because people expected that of a man. I was able to lead groups of people because I was deferred to simply for being a man, even if I had no desire to lead. Even though I did not inherently understand this, I did make assumptions based on how I was treated because I was just used to being treated that way.

There were a lot of assumptions that I had to unlearn when I began transitioning, and a lot of new ones that I needed to learn very quickly. As a woman, and especially as a transgender woman, learning the expectations and roles of women in our society was extremely important to my safety. I had to make a deliberate effort to present myself in a socially acceptable way because if I did not I was at risk.

Just as there were aspects of femininity that I took to naturally, there were a lot of aspects that I had to teach myself very quickly in order to stay safe. I began to watch how women interacted with strangers in public and semi-public places. I paid deliberate attention to how they behaved in group conversations.

Over the last three years, by deliberately picking apart the way society views women, how it treats women, and what it expects of women, and by assuming the aspects of feminine gender roles that work for me, I have discovered who I am.

It has been a wonderful journey for me and I would do it all over again given the chance.

Having picked apart what society expects of women, I then spent a lot of time trying to figure out how to present myself as just another average woman. Though the expectations I've adopted for myself are bits and pieces of what society demands of women, I am still acutely aware of what those other pieces—the ones I do not take on—are.

When I transitioned, I ultimately decided that I would just be me because using scripts just did not feel like I was being genuine to myself. If I am not feminine enough, people can deal. Even so, these scripts can be extremely helpful in passing as neurotypical—which I am not opposed to doing when needed.

I am a particularly exuberant autistic when displaying my emotions. I frequently talk loudly, gesture wildly, and generally emote in an excessive manner. This is an aspect of myself that I particularly love, and as a general rule I do not hold back on it. It is my natural state and I am okay with that, even though it stems from difficulty with emotional regulation.

It is not, however, something that is particularly welcome in society at large. Throughout my life I have been told to "tone it down" on a fairly regular basis. Because I project my emotions so strongly, people often attribute stronger emotions to me than I am actually feeling. When I am simply annoyed, I come across as angry and even confrontational. When I am mildly amused, I come across as downright giddy or silly. When I am concentrating intensely, I come across as extremely worried or anxious.

Emotional regulation is extremely hard for me, both with respect to identifying exactly what I am feeling and with expressing it at socially expected levels—especially at levels that our society considers suitable for women. Either my emotional expression is off the charts, or it is entirely turned off. There is no middle ground. This is not unusual for autistics; many of us have difficulties with emotional regulation. As a trans woman this can come across as being an "ice queen" or as overly emotional, two stereotypes that can cause me to stand out in an unsafe way.

At home and in private settings no one cares if I get too excited and raise my voice about a cute kitten on the internet. No one cares if I am happy flappy because my best friend sent me pictures. No one cares if I rant, rave, scream, and yell about someone on the news acting like a bigot. In public and semi-public places, my emotional regulation causes problems, and the pile of social skills left over from my exploration of femininity becomes a gold mine of socially acceptable scripts.

What started out as skills learned to present myself as a socially acceptable woman for personal safety have become some of my strongest, if not the strongest, and most flexible coping tools at my disposal. I may not be able to express my emotions as expected in any given situation, but I can separate my emotions from my actions and express a script instead.

In a quiet fancy environment, like an upscale restaurant, I may be anxious because of strangers and overwhelmed because of the crowd. Faced with an eventual anxiety-driven emotional overload, I can choose how I cope. I can self-regulate by stimming—bouncing my leg or chewing on my silicone toys—or I can choose a discarded script from my transition and focus my attention on playing a socially accepted role.

I am not a particularly poised person. It is a trait that I do not associate with being inherently me, but I can affect poise and project it outwardly. By focusing on being deliberately graceful in my movements, a skill I intentionally developed during my transition (and then disregarded because it just is not me), I can make being socially acceptable a stim in and of itself, as a mental challenge that satisfies my need to remain occupied. Expressing physical grace becomes a stealth stim to regulate emotional overload, allowing me to pass as neurotypical in a stressful situation that would otherwise end in meltdown.

Although I did not set out to learn scripts for neurotypical emotional expression, the scripts I learned for feminine gender expression let me express emotions in ways acceptable to the neurotypical people around me. This also becomes self-sustaining: The more I script the aspects of femininity that I personally see as useful and that are socially acceptable, the easier it becomes to script the aspects that are neurotypical.

Acceptance Over Assimilation: Gender, Autism, and Community

The first year of my transition can best be described as groping in the dark for a light switch. I knew what I wanted was out there, I knew it would illuminate aspects of myself when I found it, but I had no idea how to find it. I went through a lot of trial and error and trial by fire.

So much internalized baggage comes up when transitioning, and somehow you must figure out what is both healthy and safe. But how do you explore something you barely understand?

Navigating gender and gender roles is difficult. They are social constructs to the core, and while it is easy for me to understand that intellectually, understanding gender and gender roles intuitively is extremely difficult for me. When I realized I was autistic, that realization actually made it harder to understand gender and gender roles.

When I transitioned, I did so with certain assumptions, one of which was that I was allistic (non-autistic), though I didn't have the awareness to call myself that at the time. Transitioning with those assumptions meant that I internalized ideas about gender that did not take into account my neurodiversity. In my mind, there was a binary spectrum of gender, point Man to point Woman, as it were. That led me to believe that I must transition to "woman" and that I must behave accordingly—also based on the assumption that I am a neurotypical person.

Coming to terms with being autistic meant coming to terms with being different, in a way that I had never considered. Embracing my autistic traits meant embracing my differences and more importantly, trying to figure out what those differences were and which ones I was comfortable sharing with others. Learning about autism led to a flood of new information, which in turn led to re-examining my gender. I learned very quickly from the autistic community that there are a lot more gender options than I had ever considered.

It was a very confusing time, because I had thought the issue of my gender and the way I presented myself to the world were settled. Before I realized I was autistic, I was extremely comfortable where I was with my transition. I was a woman, and my body was well on its way to looking like I thought it should look. I was generally accepted as a woman by society as large. Misgendering was minimal, and if people thought I was unusually tall for a woman, they still thought I was a woman. I even had a safety script for explaining my height—I have a genetic thing called Marfan's Syndrome. We're tall people.

But the more I tried to examine my gender and the gender roles I was comfortable with, the more I came up feeling not quite right. Although my physical dysphoria had faded as a direct result of body-changing hormone therapy, my social dysphoria had not. I realized that despite finding comfort in being generally treated as a woman, I was not actually comfortable being perceived as a woman.

This is where autism began to shift my experience with transition away from the typical trans woman narrative. The more I examined my gender, the more I came up with nothing. The more I came up with nothing, the more my dysphoria returned. I developed a sense that maybe I was not as much of a woman as I initially thought I was. Eventually, that uncertainty become an absolute certainty.

So where does that leave me? I have been asking that question for a year now, and the best answer I can come up with is that I am a non-binary gender, I prefer feminine presentation, and I lean towards feminine gender roles, though certainly not exclusively. Beyond that, there is a wall. There is phrase spraypainted on that wall: "Gender? Nope!"

There are some things that I know for certain. I am not a man. Check. I am not a woman. Check. My physical dysphoria was absolutely linked to the presence of masculine secondary sex characteristics, and the absence of feminine ones. Check. But I was, and still am, perfectly happy with my genitalia; not necessarily a common trait among trans women, but not strictly uncommon either.

Outwardly I present myself as a woman. That is the role in society I am comfortable with, the general expectations I am comfortable with, the experiences that I relate to in a broad sense, and so forth. But while the comfort I derive from that role is very real and very important, that is not what my internal sense of self is. If we talk about how I see myself, then I am genderqueer, I am enby femme, I am non-binary. That's how I see myself in relationship to myself, how my internal dialog with myself is defined.

I have tried to define my gender, to refine what it means to me, but the more I try the more I find I cannot. Whether that is an artifact of my emotional regulation, or something different, I do not know. What is certain is that being autistic has inexorably intertwined itself with my transition. I cannot define what I am, but I can define what I am not. To me, there is a certain poetry in the symmetry: My autism creates a wall between myself and true understanding of my gender, and yet my gender exploration has broken down the walls built up around my autistic self.

The best word for me, for now, is genderqueer. It describes my orientation, it describes my gender, and it describes the gender roles that I prefer. Perhaps I could be more specific if I gave it enough time and continued to explore my gender, but I am comfortable in my queer identity and of the implied politics of acceptance over assimilation—advocating that society accept us as we are, instead of changing ourselves to fit in—that the identity comes with.

Those politics of acceptance over assimilation became the foundation for my neurodiversity activism. I am comfortable being an openly autistic person because I first learned radical acceptance from my queer community. To me, the two communities—queer and autistic—are inseparable. When push comes to shove, both are about radical acceptance and self-agency.

Exploring New Skills and Self-Expression in Radically Accepting Communities

I may not know right away whether a particular script, stim, or gender role expression feels right for me, but when I surround myself with radically accepting people, I can explore without judgement. I can make mistakes and do things that are uncomfortable. That freedom lets me figure out what works for me and what doesn't.

When I can do that, the things that "feel right" become natural expressions of myself. Everything else naturally falls by the wayside. This more than anything else has allowed me to come into my own, both with regards to my gender and my autistic traits. It works so well that I can use it to practice expressions of autistic traits or expressions of my gender, and transition them into comfortable daily use, much like I did with my gender.

For example, if I see something that looks like a particularly satisfying stim, I have two communities where I can expect that regardless of what the stim is, it will be accepted: the queer community and the autistic community. This gives me access to private and semi-private places to try out the new stim.

If I enjoy it, if I am comfortable with it, I try it in more public spaces. If I am not comfortable with it, the stim usually just stops because I am not getting the comfort or sensory experience that I was hoping for.

On the gender expression side of things, this is how I became comfortable with leggings. For two years, I was adamant that I would not like leggings because they showed off too much of my body. I tried them out in the queer community, and found that they weren't so bad after all. As I became more comfortable with leggings, more of them found their way into my wardrobe and I began wearing them under skirts in public. My skirts got shorter, and eventually I reached the point where I wanted to wear leggings, my skirts were all in the laundry, and I didn't think twice about putting them on and going out in public. Now, leggings are one of my staple wardrobe items.

This has become my go-to process for new self-expression. If I want to find out whether something is "me" or should be discarded, I turn to my radically accepting communities first, because it is through them that I find acceptance and self-acceptance.

Solving Problems with Skills from Multiple Identities

Some problems are complex, and I need knowledge and skills from multiple areas of life to solve them. Until I transitioned I had little to no emotional regulation. I was frequently compartmentalizing my emotions to the point of depersonalization. Learning and sometimes deliberately studying what emotional displays our society finds acceptable in women versus men has led me to a much healthier expression of emotion.

Although my transition improved my emotional regulation by broadening what was acceptable for me to express, it wasn't until I took what I'd learned and applied it to my autistic traits that I really blossomed emotionally.

I had always believed myself to be a particularly hypo-empathetic person and years of therapists have worked hard to rid me of that problem. It turns out I am hyper-empathetic, I just did not know how to handle it in a healthy way. Empathy would overwhelm me and I would depersonalize. Spending time in the autistic community introduced me to the idea of hyperempathy and allowed me to look at my emotions from a different angle. It is that different perspective that opened me to new coping techniques.

It took knowing and understanding myself as a woman and knowing and understanding myself as an autistic to really understand my emotions.

Learning Autism-Specific Techniques for Executive Dysfunction

Every coping tool I developed in the first thirty-five years of my life, I developed without knowing I was autistic, by identifying, isolating, and transferring skills developed for other things. The cognitive-behavioral therapy techniques I learned for anxiety, for example, have helped me avoid more than one meltdown, and the stimming I use to keep my OCD at bay can help me with sensory self-regulation.

Only in the last year or so have I actively been learning coping techniques specifically to deal with my autistic nature. One of the most useful skillsets I've learned is for coping with autism-related executive dysfunction—difficulty with self-regulating, planning, and executing tasks, which many autistic people struggle with.

Before diagnosis, I spent my life struggling with the belief that I was inherently lazy, that I was a procrastinator. Because I didn't know I was autistic, I saw my struggles as moral failings. It was extremely unhealthy and played a significant role in my life-long depression.

As a student in high school I failed multiple classes, despite being labeled as gifted, because I simply refused to do a lot of the homework. When I was interested in something, when it excited and energized me, it increased my ability to do it well. But I hated math, and without that interest and excitement I could not convince myself to do the work. The longer I delayed working on it, the harder it was to do, and eventually I learned that it was less stressful to refuse from the start. Adults and even my peers treated this as a moral failure, assuming that because I was smart enough to do the tasks, the fault must lie with my willingness to do the work—even though it was actually a consequence of executive dysfunction.

As a working adult I struggled less, largely because I was regularly in a position to delegate. With a desire for routines and predictability, I was able to codify company rules and policies into my work routine, and at jobs where I was not physically limited by disability, I thrived and reached management positions quickly. But I still struggled, and my upward mobility was ultimately limited. Despite my ability to work within company structures, I was frequently late to work, late returning from lunch, late to complete projects, and just generally not very good at managing my time.

This is not an unfamiliar story for autistics. Executive function is something many of us struggle with, and being unproductive in a productivity-driven society is heavily stigmatized. Many of us don't realize it might have a neurological cause, and we end up trying to cope without knowing what is actually wrong. It is no surprise then that we fail to successfully cope. It wasn't until after I was diagnosed that I even knew executive function—or rather dysfunction—was something that could be coped with. All I know is that even with a planner and Google Calendar I was horrible at managing my day to day life.

Learning that I was autistic, and that executive dysfunction is common in autism, opened doors with my therapist. With her outside perspective on my life and her knowledge of relevant tricks and tips, I've been gradually incorporating executive function management into all of my routines. I still struggle, but less so than before, and I continue to get better at managing my life—so much so that I have started applying my executive dysfunction management tools to other aspects of my life, especially physical disability.

Executive Function Management as a Physical Accommodation

Now that I know I am autistic, I can take coping skills I've learned for autistic traits and apply them to other areas of my life as well.

I am physically disabled. I have a broken back; one of my vertebra is in two pieces and never fused. This causes a lot of problems, among them pain radiating up my back and loss of feeling radiating down my right leg. The longer I spend at any given task the longer I have to spend recovering. After an hour at a task, I have to spend more time recovering than working.

I used to love to cook full meals over the course of several hours. When I broke my back, I lost that ability. Since I could no longer spend hours in the kitchen I simply stopped cooking. Microwavable meals become the norm.

When I was diagnosed autistic and learned about executive dysfunction, I started bullet journaling to manage my day-to-day activities. With my therapist's help, I changed how I viewed tasks, breaking big tasks down into smaller, shorter ones. I now approach life as a series of many short tasks with frequent breaks between them, which allows me to handle large tasks without overwhelming my executive function abilities.

As a byproduct, I found my back hurting less frequently. Although some of my reduction in pain was due to physical therapy and better pain management, a large portion of it was because executive function management gives me what I need to perform physical tasks—short bursts of activity with frequent breaks.

When I realized I could actively apply the executive dysfunction management to my time in the kitchen, I made several changes. The first was to take more frequent, smaller trips to the grocery store, purchasing only what I would use to cook that day. The immediate benefit of shorter trips was that I was in a lot less pain. Shopping only for the meal at hand meant I could cook on the same day I went grocery shopping. Additionally, less food went bad from sitting in the fridge due to unexpected bad days where cooking was impossible. This freed up extra money, if not a lot, that could be spent on convenience.

The second change I made was to buy pre-made items for some foods. A salad is a salad; it doesn't matter to me if I make it home or purchase it premade because it tastes the same regardless. But a salad is also a lot of prep work spent hunched over the counter, which aggravates my disability and limits my time in the kitchen.

The third change I made was to increase efficiency, something that also stood out to me when learning how to manage executive dysfunction. Applying efficiency to cooking means cooking in bulk and using recipes with ingredients that do not require physical prep work. Instead of cooking for the night and maybe lunch the next day, I now cook for three or four meals at a time, sometimes more. The added efficiency is multiplied in recipes like crockpot chili that largely consist of beans from a can or only need to be set to soak.

There are plenty of spoonie resources that suggest prepping vegetables the night before you cook them, spreading the task out so that not everything is done at once on the day of cooking. But that still left me bumping against my physical limitations. Thinking about vegetable prep from an executive function perspective, however, extended the amount of time I could spend cooking by breaking it into smaller steps. Rather than thinking about prepping all the vegetables the night before, I broke it down into individual types of vegetables. Just carrots. Just potatoes. Just broccoli. Sometimes, I even break it down to individual vegetables. A carrot. A potato. One head of broccoli.

Suddenly the task is neither overwhelming nor is it physically demanding. Five minutes of cooking is significantly different than thirty minutes of cooking, especially when there are ten minutes between bursts of activity.

The most useful lesson I took from executive function management was the value of breaking things down into small steps. Now when I find myself struggling physically the first thing I ask myself is not how can I physically accommodate to meet my needs, but rather: What can I do to change how I view this task and to break it into manageable pieces? This has become such second nature that I'm now better at physically accommodating my disability using executive dysfunction management than I am at actually managing my executive dysfunction for its own sake.

It is not a perfect system, but it is better than what I had before. I am not cooking regularly, but I am cooking more often. As I get better at managing my executive dysfunction I find that I am more and more capable of meeting my physical needs. All it took was a change of perspective on how to accommodate those needs.

Identifying, Isolating, and Transferring Scripts and Skills (Refrain)

As someone who did not know that they are autistic until well into adulthood, most of my life was spent coping with my autistic traits without knowing that I was coping with them. Those coping skills had to come from somewhere, and it turns out they frequently come from other identities.

For thirty-three years I managed my autistic traits, unknowingly, using skills I learned to manage depression, anxiety, OCD, and multiple physical disabilities. Learning I was autistic increased my ability to identify and isolate skills from other areas of my life and apply them to being autistic, such as when I use discarded scripts from my transition to help with emotional regulation. I can use my radically accepting queer and autistic communities to test and explore new scripts, skills, and expressions of identity. Learning I was autistic also opened the door to learning autism-specific skills that I can then use for other identities or disabilities, like using executive function management skills to help manage physical disability.

Of all the coping tools that I have, the ability to identify and isolate coping tools from one identity and transfer them for use in other situations is the most powerful tool at my disposal. The more I do it, the easier it becomes.

As a late diagnosed autistic, I am certain this is the only reason I have gotten as far as I have in life. I wish I had known all my life I am autistic, but at least I have this as a silver lining.

ABOUT THE AUTHOR

Samantha Hack is a multiply disabled neurodiversity and disability activist, student, blogger, and freelance writer from Houston, Texas. Samantha attends the University of Houston-Downtown as a sociology and psychology undergraduate where she focuses her studies on autistic culture and communication. You can find Samantha's blog, Sparrows and Penguins, at http://www.sparrowsandpenguins.com. Some of Samantha's more recent personal achievements include administration for a multi-faith spiritual support group, sitting as a panelist on intersex and transgender healthcare for Baylor College of Medicine, co-founding an autistic women's support group, and founding a non-binary support group.

AUTISTIC NAVIGATION OF CHRONIC ILLNESS, MENTAL ILLNESS, AND HEALTHCARE

Amythest Schaber

The doctor enters the room in the back of the clinic without knocking. I sit up on the examination table and press my palm to the side of my face, trying to breathe through the pain, trying to find my words. I usually avoid walk-in doctors. But it's a holiday today so my regular doctor isn't available, and there's no way I can make it until tomorrow.

"Oh, hello—why is the light off? I need the light to see the computer." She flicks on the humming overhead light and drops into the seat in front of the glowing screen.

I'm not sure what to say here. Her voice demands an answer. Her question is not rhetorical. Using words is proving difficult. "The light was bothering me, so I turned it off," I say.

"What?" she asks loudly, turning her head towards me but not taking her eyes off of the computer screen. I start to speak again, each word hard won, but she cuts me off—"What? I can't hear you!"

I repeat myself.

"So why was the light off?" The doctor seems very focused on the light and I start to feel apprehensive. My husband Marvin is sitting nearby on a chair in the corner. He looks to me, wanting to know if he should step in. I indicate no. I've decided to stick it out, get some pain medication, and go home.

"Fluorescent lights hurt me." So does talking. I can feel my panic building as the nerve pain in my lower job throbs. I've been waiting so long. I just want to go home.

"But why?" she presses.

"I'm autistic," I say. Now her whole body turns towards me. Her eyes travel up and down my body and then back up again.

"You were diagnosed with autism?" Her tone is unmistakable. It's that old familiar, disbelief.

"Yes. I am autistic," I repeat.

"How did that happen? Who diagnosed you?" The strangeness of her question throws me off. How did that happen? I was born. Marvin shifts in his seat, frowning, wanting to say something but letting me speak for myself.

"Doctor Todd Mason at the ABLE clinic. He diagnosed me. But that's not why I'm here." I say it as firmly as I can.

"Ah. Okay. Well, then why are you here?" The doctor finally concedes.

I explain that I recently had my wisdom teeth extracted, but that I've been healing slowly. I just need a refill of my pain medication to hold me over until I can see the dental surgeon again.

I show her my other medications. I tell her how much I've been taking and what my pain level is out of ten. She asks a question or two about the surgery. I think that maybe we're past the "autism thing" now, so I relax a little. No such luck. She pauses typing out the prescription on the computer and looks over with a challenging look on her face.

"You don't look like you have autism to me."

Marvin straightens in his chair. I fold my hands in my lap. We shoot each other identical glances and I pause to think before I answer. Carefully. Because I need help, and this doctor can help me, but she might just choose not to if I make a wrong step.

"There aren't... There aren't actually any physical indicators of autism."

"Then how did you get this diagnosis?" Her facial expression speaks of slyness, as if she thinks she's got me there. Like I'm going to suddenly burst out laughing and admit I've been joking with her.

"Well, specialists look for autistic traits in different areas." I feel myself losing my words. The world vibrates. The lights flicker and burn me. Pain throbs. "Like, I have narrow-but-deep interests. And I have sensory integration issues, and I have some cognitive disabilities, also. I can't tell time from clocks with hands. So the doctor who diagnosed me looked for these traits, these autistic 'symptoms,' and then put them together. That is how autism is diagnosed. Looking for the traits."

As I'm speaking the doctor's expression shifts from confused to annoyed, and then to totally disinterested. She has stopped listening. As she prints off the prescription and signs her name she manages to get the last word in on the topic, one last jab of invalidation, one last challenge.

"Well, you don't seem like you have autism to me."

I leave the office feeling distraught in a way that's hard to name and hurts deep inside. As an autistic person diagnosed in adulthood, I am familiar with the ache of invalidation. As an autistic person whose ability to sometimes pass for neurotypical is capable of fooling some people, in some situations, I now expect disbelief and arguments when I talk about being autistic.

In my experiences, doctors have fallen into three general categories:

◆ Those that are largely ignorant about autism spectrum disorders and who do not believe that I am autistic

◆ Those who believe that I am autistic but are also still largely uneducated about autism spectrum disorders

◆ And those do believe that I am autistic and who have at least some correct knowledge about autism

That last type is by far the rarest.

I know that I didn't "seem autistic" to that doctor. There was a failing there, but it wasn't mine. There is widespread ignorance and miseducation about autism among doctors, healthcare providers, and even autism "experts." But access to appropriate healthcare is a basic right, and everyone will need healthcare at some point in their lives.

So what is an autistic person to do? And what of those of us who are sick, mentally or physically ill, or who have comorbid or co-existing physiological conditions?

We have to take care of ourselves.

I am autistic. I come from an autistic family parented by a single autistic woman. My family existed at or below the poverty level and moved houses and cities many times. I was also a girl. I think that all of these things contributed to my neurotype and impairments being missed in my childhood. I was not assessed and formally diagnosed with autism until I was twenty-two.

I am chronically ill. I was born with a genetic condition that affects how my body functions in two major ways. The first is that my body produces faulty collagen. The joints in my body are weakened and can sublux or dislocate with very little force. The second is that my body's autonomic functions—those vital background operations that involve every organ and system in your body—simply don't go right. My body has difficulty regulating everything from my temperature to my digestion to my blood pressure (as it turns out, you can't stay conscious if your blood pressure is too low, never mind sitting or standing up).

I also have myalgic encephalomyelitis, which is more widely known as chronic fatigue syndrome, and which is exactly as much fun as it sounds. My symptoms have impaired me since I was eighteen years old.

I am physically disabled. My collagen disorder causes widespread joint pain (although I am bendier than others, it hurts just as much when something pops out of place). I use mobility aids, have adapted my home, and take medications for my pain.

I am mentally ill. I have had OCD and a dissociation disorder since early childhood. I went through a very severe autistic burnout when I was twenty-two. During that time I experienced paranoia and hallucinations alongside severe OCD symptoms.

Six years ago I started seeking out medical treatment and professional opinions for health issues that cropped up in my late teens. Those issues have been getting worse since I turned twenty, although I have as much difficulty getting taken seriously today.

Six years ago I started spending a lot of time in doctor's offices. A lot of time dealing with receptionists, visiting pharmacies, and fighting for referrals from specialists. For six years I have been making appointments and getting labs, tests, and blood draw after blood draw done.

For six years I have been visiting the emergency room multiple times a year. Last winter the illness of the season was recurrent double pneumonia. The winter before that, it was recurrent bladder and kidney infections.

I have lost consciousness on the sidewalk, on a staircase, in a walk-in clinic, at college, at the grocery store, in parking lots and parks. I have had ambulances called against my strong wishes and had EMTs descend on me, ignoring my protestations or explanations. I have had strangers put their hands on my body. I have had strangers speak over me with the confidence of people who think they know better than you do.

₂❧

At this point in my life, I am professionally ill. By that I mean, with tongue in cheek, that I spend an unfortunate amount of time and energy working on managing my "case." In the way that my peers have jobs, careers, and professions, I manage my healthcare and take care of my body. I treat its constantly shifting kaleidoscope of symptoms and try to improve my quality of life. I work on learning how to use my body to the best of its ability.

Between this full-time job and trying to fit a life worth living into the margins, there is no time or energy left for me to pursue a traditional career. Hence, I am professionally ill. I can't change it. I just have to accept it, again and again, because the process of acceptance is not linear.

Although I'm still learning and figuring things out, I've been doing this a while. I've learned some ways to get noticed, listened to, believed. And still, I would classify over half of my experiences with the healthcare system as unproductive or unhelpful. Worst of all, I have had painful and traumatizing experiences at the hands of people who were supposed to help me.

The trap-laden maze of the healthcare system is difficult and dangerous for anyone to navigate. Expecting people who are already fatigued, ill, or in pain to navigate it is unrealistic. Yet here we are, in offices and hospitals all over the world every day, standing toe-to-toe with everyone from apathetic receptionists to arrogant surgeons. The cruel reality is that ill people have to fight simply to receive the quality of care that every person deserves, and autistic people who are chronically ill, mentally ill, or both have additional barriers and prejudices we have to fight against.

❧

When I was twenty-one I was going through a severe autistic burn-out. One night I was desperate and pained enough to seek out help at the emergency room. I was admitted to the emergency psychiatric wing for an overnight stay. A doctor would assess me in the morning. At that time I was undiagnosed, and no one knew what to make of me.

I didn't want to stay overnight. I had wanted to see a doctor. Since the doctor had gone home, I decided to go home for the night and come back in the morning. I wasn't an immediate threat to myself or anyone else, I just couldn't function and would slip into catatonic states where I didn't move or speak. But the head nurse used a euphemism when he asked me if I was suicidal.

He asked, "Are you going to hurt yourself?"

At the time I was engaging in a lot of injurious stimming. I took his words literally and answered "yes."

When I tried to explain later in the conversation that I had misunderstood and was not suicidal, he acted as if I were lying to try to leave. He pushed and pushed until Marvin and I were unsettled enough to concede to me staying overnight.

As part of my agreeing to stay overnight, the head nurse promised I would be able to keep my iPad. Besides being a prized possession and comfort item, my tablet is loaded with a writing app and the AAC apps that I use to communicate. It was a valid accommodation for an autistic person who was barely verbal at the time.

I also had Marvin help me insist that I would not take any medication whatsoever until I was seen by the doctor in the morning. To this, both the head nurse and the nurse in charge of administering medication agreed.

Our requests for accommodation of my disabilities were valid. We were reasonable, cooperative patients who asked all the right questions and advocated for appropriate accommodations and care. Marvin assured me that it was only ten hours apart, promised he'd be back as soon as they let him in. They let him out of the wing.

The moment that Marvin was gone, the head nurse's attitude took a turn. The first thing to go was my iPad. I held on as best as I could, typing frantically to try to explain, and using my voice as best I could. But I couldn't hold on tight enough, and it was taken and locked in a small locker for "security reasons."

After being told that I could keep my underwear on underneath the hospital gown they put me in, I was instructed to take it off. I was threatened into taking two pills from a tiny paper cup, an anti-anxiety medication and a sleep aid.

I was forced into a cold room with a cot in it. When the curtains over the cut-out in the door were drawn, the windowless room was so dark that I couldn't see anything.

I was shaking from fear and from cold, because my dysautonomia impedes my body's ability to produce enough of its own heat. When the nurse on the night shift would check up on me I would beg for another blanket. She ignored me, like I hadn't said anything.

I hallucinated all night. I didn't sleep. I cried as quietly as I could.

When the morning came and the shift changed over, things got better. A young nurse checked in on me and found me on the cot, rocking and catatonic. She felt my hands and bare feet and came back with a heated blanket.

She kindly asked me if rocking my body was helping me feel better, and when I nodded yes, she let me do it. Later she made sure I received some breakfast because I almost got passed over by the meal cart.

The experience changed me. This is the first time that I have written about it. As an autistic person, my brain quickly makes connections and is sometimes too good at learning and anticipating patterns from traumatic experiences. The trauma from that time is difficult to deal with.

I don't know if I could bring myself to access emergency psychiatric services if I needed them right now. I know there are other autistic folk who been similarly mistreated and who feel the same way.

I wish I had better advice here for autistic people in the same situation. What I have is this: You have the right to access healthcare and to be healthy. You deserve to be respected and have your needs acknowledged. There will be bad staff, bad professionals. But there will be good ones, too.

The nurse on the morning shift who brought me a blanket and made sure I got breakfast. The doctor I saw later at that emergency room visit who sent me on to an early intervention program for people with psychotic disorders. The psychiatrist at the early intervention program who told me that I had autistic traits and encouraged me to seek assessment. The team of professionals that later diagnosed me with autism.

My hospitalization was a horrible experience that hurt me. It was a dark and scary stretch on the path that brought me to my diagnosis and to the self-awareness that I continue to cultivate—but it was still a stretch on that path. If I hadn't gone to the emergency room that night, I might gotten to that point in another way, but perhaps not. I was in deep distress and largely non-functional at the time. I needed help, and I asked for it. At times, I demanded it. Eventually, I even received it.

ॐ

Yet it's not uncommon for doctors and other healthcare professionals to feel threatened or become suspicious around people who are assertive, or who advocate for their autistic needs being met, like the walk-in doctor who refused to believe I was autistic, or the head nurse at my emergency room visit.

I have had doctors misjudge what was happening when I would look to my husband for help answering questions. They snappily demand that I alone answer their questions, and only verbal answers will do. I've had doctors tell me to put down the list of points that I prepared to talk about beforehand, as if I'm in a closed book exam and they caught me with a cheat sheet.

These reactions to the coping methods autistic folk use to organise and manage our interactions with doctors are expressions of anti-autistic ableism. Practitioners often assume every patient will function like a non-autistic person, and apply common misconceptions about how someone acts when they are sincere or lying, genuine or "faking," with harmful results.

Many culturally common beliefs about what liars will or won't do are wrong. Using eye contact—a contentious point for many autistic folks—as an example, "common knowledge" says that people who won't or can't make eye contact are surely lying. This is wrong, of course, even for non-autistic people. But these beliefs persist.

Many autistic folk have difficulty accessing effective mental health resources when we need to, even once we are correctly diagnosed, and even if we have healthcare coverage. Many psychiatrists, psychologists, and therapists are not comfortable working with autistic people. Those who are comfortable enough to work with us are more often than not miseducated about autistic people.

This is due to many factors. The field of autism study and research is relatively new, and with some exceptions, most research on autism is conducted by non-autistic researchers, without input from autistic people. Not for lack of effort on the autistic community's part, autistic people historically have not been asked why we do things, what our experiences are, or what we need, and outsider observations are often trusted over our firsthand accounts. This has resulted in inaccurate ideas and biased research.

Even when good information about autism is available, healthcare providers may still be underinformed or misinformed. Many mental health professionals go through their entire education having only read a paragraph on autism, once, in a unit on early childhood disorders. Older professionals will have been taught now-outdated information about autism (if they learned anything about autism at all).

The result of all this is that mental health providers may have beliefs about autism that are inaccurate and harmful. They may believe that autistic people lack "Theory of Mind," the ability to understand that people have beliefs, desires, and thoughts of their own, and that other people are their own people. I have yet to meet an autistic adult who doesn't know or understand that other people have their own thoughts and feelings, although I have encountered many non-autistic people who disbelieve autistic people's thoughts and feelings by default.

Some mental health providers underestimate the abilities of autistic people, particularly nonverbal autistic people. Some providers are resistant to helping autistic people with communication difficulties access alternative methods of communication, even though communication is a basic right, and every autistic person should have access to and instruction in methods of communication that work best for them.

Some mental health providers believe that autistic people don't desire social interaction or need relationships. That autistic people don't feel emotion or experience the same range of feelings as non-autistic people do. That we lack empathy. That we can't love.

These ideas are common and harmful, and impede our access to mental health services and our ability to open up when we need to. How can we trust a therapist who believes that we aren't whole people, that we're emotionless and empty—or that if we do have emotions and relationships, we can't be autistic?

The good news is that things are changing slowly. Doctors being trained now are often introduced to autism spectrum disorders, even if it is often a brief and shallow introduction. Groups like AASPIRE (the Academic Autistic Spectrum Partnership In Research and Education) are working to create partnerships between the academic community and the autistic community.

In the meantime, though, it can fall to us to educate providers. If your doctor or therapist reveals that they believe something untrue about autistic people, or about you, you can speak up. They may not receive it well, but they might, and by sharing your experience you may be able correct inaccurate ideas.

What you say can be as simple as "That hasn't been my experience." Or, "Well, in my experience, and in the experience of the author of this book I've read, this is what has been helpful." If you are lucky, you will be working with someone whose professional integrity and desire to help overpower the human desire to be right. And if you are not, you may be able to switch providers.

Autistic people often have at least one co-occurring neurological condition or disorder which affects our health and wellness. Often these conditions are as or more misunderstood than autism. When healthcare providers are ignorant of these conditions, or misinformed about them, they may misunderstand or misdiagnose us, preventing us from getting needed help.

Many autistic people have alexithymia, difficulty with or inability to identify or express emotions or feelings. Alexithymia can also cause atypical interoception, or altered awareness of one's internal body sensations. It can contribute to the monotonous voice or flat affect that many autistic people have.

A doctor not trained to know how non-autistic people present when distressed may not recognize distress in an autistic person. They may even be suspicious of someone with a flat affect who claims to be in pain. When someone cannot describe their symptoms or specify any more than "I feel bad," doctors may feel at a loss.

Sensory processing disorder can cause sensations that are not painful or aversive to other people to be painful and aversive to us. Healthcare practitioners have mistaken symptoms of my sensory processing disorder for hypochondria, attention-seeking, and generalized anxiety disorder. When we express pain or aversion, they may tell us "you're too sensitive," "that doesn't hurt," "you shouldn't be able to feel that," or "that can't possibly be bothering you." They've interpreted my flinching away from a light shined in my eyes or from the clammy touch of a strange hand as anxiety. My experience goes disbelieved because it isn't their experience. They may think or say, "It doesn't bother me, how could it bother you?" (Even though we are supposed to be the ones who can't tell that others have experiences that differ from our own.)

Central auditory processing disorder causes difficulty recognizing and interpreting sounds despite normal hearing. My central auditory processing disorder has been mistaken for being hard of hearing. My hearing was even tested once, which was unnecessary, as I can hear more than most people. And almost everyone with an auditory processing disorder has been accused of being a "selective listener," i.e. deliberately refusing to pay attention—even though, of course, we are often trying as hard as we can to understand what we hear.

Autistic people also often have motor differences: Our bodies move and work differently than non-autistic people's bodies do. Doctors often don't know what to do with this. My stimming has been interpreted as everything except what it actually is—a natural method of accommodation that helps regulate sensory input, allows for better processing, and can act as expression. There are doctors (so-called specialists in autism, even) who believe that stimming is somehow harmful or impedes development.

For healthcare professionals to provide useful health care to us, whether physical or mental healthcare, they need a foundation of basic knowledge of autism and related co-conditions. Unfortunately, building this foundation usually falls to us and our allies, instead of to the educators who ought to be ensuring that medical professionals know what they should know about our needs, or to healthcare practitioners themselves.

If you want to disclose your autism to your healthcare team—and you may not have to, if you don't want to—or if they already know about it, you will very likely have to do some educating. When it comes to that education, be fearless with information. Sharing specific examples of what you are talking about and explaining how something affects you personally can also help create a picture of you and your needs.

It doesn't have to be eloquent or detailed. An explanation of stimming could be, "This is a difficult environment for me and stimming helps me self-regulate," or "I feel better when I can move my hands like this."

You also don't have to come up with everything yourself. There are many great resources you can find online, by and for autistic people, to explain what autism is and how it affects you. You can print out Autism 101 articles or FAQ pages relevant to you and your experiences, and give them to your doctors. Don't be afraid to correct any misconceptions that your doctors may have. You should feel free to offer information and examples of your experiences to help your doctors understand. This doesn't always work—but when it does, it can be incredibly helpful.

Something that I knew as a general concept, but that took me some time to fully internalize, is that your doctors work for you.

In theory, you have the right to change doctors or to ask for a second opinion. If you feel like you are not being respected, that a doctor isn't listening, or that you are not receiving the care you need, or if you don't feel safe, that is a valid reason to go somewhere else or see a different doctor.

In practice, this can be messy and difficult. Doctors are human. Many autistic people have difficulty with communication or have been abused or mistreated, so standing up to an authority figure who hold power over them can prove challenging. Even when not challenging, it may just feel really awkward.

After we moved houses, I took the opportunity (and used it as an excuse) to switch doctors. My previous general practitioner was awful to work with. At his best, he was generally unhelpful. At his worst, I received such pearls of wisdom as "Many women have strange symptoms with no physical cause, because women are so emotional. It's very normal and not much can be done," "Most joint pain is caused by depression, so you should be sure to take long walks in the sunshine every day," and "I feel strongly that you are depressed, and would feel better if you had a feminine hobby to keep your mind occupied, such as knitting."

Marvin was there for that one and can attest to the nonsense and general bad form by that doctor. We often repeat variations of that last quote, in dry humour, after encounters with particularly sexist doctors.

Because I have now switched doctors, I can laugh about that awful doctor. At the time, though, it was incredibly frustrating, and the invalidation was devastating.

My current family doctor is open-minded, reasonable, and curious. He treats me with respect and, over time, has come to trust my understanding of my body and to take my input into consideration.

I acknowledge that I speak from a place of privilege on the topic, because I am Canadian and have access to our universal healthcare system. If I lived in a country without universal healthcare, I might be constrained by my financial situation or by the selection of doctors or hospitals my insurance would cover. But if you have the means, seeking out another doctor or a second opinion can help you find someone who respects and listens to you.

We often have to take care of ourselves. In a perfect world, patients could entrust their healthcare to the system and be confident their needs will be met. In a perfect world, doctors and healthcare professionals would have at least a 101-level knowledge of autism and neuro-atypicality. Sadly, that world doesn't exist yet.

But you live in this world, and you need care now. We can't totally trust or rely on the healthcare system or on professionals. Although it isn't fair, it is true that you need to be looking out for yourself.

You should feel empowered to do your own research, to request appointments with your healthcare professionals, and to learn about any medications or treatments recommended to you before you start them. You should feel free to prepare any notes or scripts you need beforehand.

In the case of your health and well-being, your safety outweighs the comfort of non-autistic people. That goes for nurses, doctors, and specialists, too. It's more important to make your needs known and for everyone to have the information they need to provide you with appropriate care.

I have to fight my growing mistrust of the healthcare system and find motivation to keep fighting for myself. I want to survive. It's hard work, and it's an unfair burden, but it is worth doing.

When I was first referred to my current internist, I was nervous and excited. A specialist in internal medicine, this new doctor was my hope. I needed to find something that would help me raise my low blood pressure and control my dysautonomia symptoms. I wanted to feel better. And to make sure this happened, I wanted to be a co-operative patient and not give my new internist any reason to regret taking my case.

The first medication that the internist tried me on didn't help my blood pressure. I finished my trial of the drug without feeling a positive difference, only unpleasant side effects.

By this time, years of negative experiences had informed my feelings. I tried to be logical but still worried. I worried that, if I reported that this first medication had not helped at all, my internist would give up. That I would be seen as being too difficult, a "tough case." That I would be relegated to the wastebasket of the incurably-ill-and-hysterical. It had happened before.

Marvin talked through my upcoming doctor's appointment with me. I prepared a script. I reminded myself of what I wanted and that I had a right to adequate care.

My internist took it like any decent doctor would—he believed me. He explained that there was another drug that we could try. He explained that he had only one other patient on this medication. That it was rare and that our pharmacy might have to order it in. That it was expensive, and that there might be some strange side-effects.

After explaining that, he asked if I really wanted to try it. He seemed ambivalent himself, but he let me decide.

I said yes. He wrote the prescription. Things changed for the better.

That medication was a wonderful addition to my life and does everything I wanted it to. It's true—the strange scalp tingles and spontaneous shudders are pretty weird, and being on a rare medication can be a headache. But being able to stay conscious and upright? That's pretty great.

I humbly encourage you to keep trying, too. To be honest about your experiences. To feel empowered to take your rightful place as the director of your health and the final authority on your well-being.

It's an unfortunate thing that truly good doctors are in the minority, but they are out there. You can tell them by the way that they listen and respect your decisions.

Good doctors acknowledge their patient's personhood, regardless of disability, impairment, or illness. Everyone deserves a good doctor and help when and how they need it. I hope that will happen for you.

By sharing our stories we are creating opportunities for doctors to become better. We make paths for the patients who come after us and generate awareness and understanding. Let us be brave when we can.

❦

I know that I will have more opportunities to fight for myself in the future. I know that when I try to navigate the world of physical illness, ignorance of autism will impede my care. I know that when I want to seek mental health care I will run into professionals who doubt my autism diagnosis. They have insisted that I am just shy, just quirky, and will do so again. I have to remember who I am.

I will meet people in power over me who try to convince me that I don't know myself. I am autistic, and chronically ill, and physically disabled, and mentally ill. I am all of these things and that is okay. Even though some people don't want to believe in people like me, that's okay. Depending on the space I am standing in, aspects of me are invisible and visible by turns. But they are still there.

I also know that I deserve adequate care. That I am worthy of consideration and respect. You deserve these things, too. I hope you believe me, even when you're up against another wall, another hurdle, another battle.

Just by being visible and insisting on who I am and what I need, I am advocating for myself and other autistic people. If you want it, that's for you too.

We don't yet live in a perfect world, or even a very good one. Not for people like me, disabled and ill. The system that is supposed to help us is broken on top of flawed, but I think it can be fixed.

I have slipped between the cracks. I've been invisible. But I've also carved out a place for myself and stood my ground to defend it. I've found some good doctors to depend on and I'm figuring out how to get what I need.

I will keep working towards that dream of a system that has healing for everyone and that doesn't hurt. So many of us are working towards that. In the meantime, I keep trying to learn. I keep doing what I need to do to survive. I give you permission to do the same.

ABOUT THE AUTHOR

Amythest Schaber is a Métis, Autistic, and multiply disabled writer, public speaker, artist, and activist. She was officially diagnosed with Autism Spectrum Disorder in July of 2013. You can find her Ask an Autistic video series at https://youtube.com/user/neurowonderful.

THE SPECTRUM AND DEPRESSION: FOUR STORIES

M. KELTER

The Lamp

July, 2006

Mom calls. In her willfully cheery voice, she says, "We're coming into town for a visit!"

I look around my crappy, shoe-box sized apartment and think this may not be a good idea. They've never seen my current abode.

"I'm sick," I tell her.

"We'll bring medicine," she replies.

"High fever. Very contagious."

"I'll make soup!"

The call ends. I mentally organize liquor store options.

Next day, mom and dad arrive. They look around the apartment. Their faces collapse.

The room is dark. There are no lamps. No television. The only furniture in the living room is a two-person couch. Mostly, though, they stare at the wall where I've nailed blankets over the windows. I have done this at every place I've ever lived due to a painful aversion to lights...yet it still confuses them. They stare and stare at those blankets. Attempts to explain my sensory aversions never sink in, probably because they don't fit their mental cookie cutter for what my life is supposed to be like. (The cookie cutter, from what I can tell, is normal-shaped.)

Dad takes a seat on the small couch, stares at the back of his hand. I take a seat on the floor, stare at my shoes. Mom walks over to the fridge, opens it; it's empty. She opens the freezer...it's stuffed with a dozen or so frozen rectangles. She closes the freezer, looks into the fridge again, asks, "Where's the rest of your food?"

I scratch my head, think that one over and say "I don't understand the question."

She sits next to dad, fake smiles her way through the awkward silence.

Mentally, I dig around, try to access the small talk files. I line up a few good options, pepper them with questions. They answer. It goes quiet again. Mom fake smiles.

At one point, dad bristles and says, "You're living like some kind of hermit." Which is progress. The year before he called me a "shut-in." I think "hermit" is definitely an upgrade; kinda feels like we're bonding.

I give him a thumbs-up. He sighs.

I definitely understand their reaction. At their place, they're used to perpetual lights and sounds; day and night, they keep televisions going full blast and a radio spurting out talk radio. At my place, they probably feel like hostages in a sensory deprivation tank.

Also, mom recently described visiting some of my cousins who are close in age to me. They're all bright, happy people living in large homes filled with Normal Stuff and Expensive Crap. Mom was impressed. I think she can't help but compare my situation to theirs. I think it makes her sad.

I never know how to explain to them: I'm not thrilled with my life either. I'm depressed, in therapy. I was recently diagnosed as being on the autism spectrum. Which is a positive development; it helps make sense of a lot of experiences. But the information was a lot to absorb. I don't know how to re-organize my sense of self, manage the depression and start living a more fulfilling existence, all at the same time. I just know that if things can get better, my life still won't look like my parents' definition of success. There's just too much distance between us.

So, I don't say anything. We just sit, stare, pass around small talk questions and answers.

Mom keeps looking over at the wall-blankets. Finally, she asks, "Why don't you let us buy you a nice set of curtains? It can be a house-warming gift."

"No thanks."

"But with curtains, you can keep it dark...they'll just give you more options, let you change the lighting whenever you need to."

"That's nice, but no thank you."

Mom thinks it over, says, "If I can't buy you curtains, can I at least buy you a floor lamp?"

I could easily say no, but it seems like a simple way to make them happy. A little token gesture from time to time never hurts.

I say, "Let's do it."

We load up, go to a big store. We stare at floor lamps. Mom says, "I found it! This is the one you need!"

It's the largest, brightest lamp in the store. Maybe of all time.

"This is the lamp that I don't want," I tell her. "In the entire world. This is the one. You found it."

We look at others, compare/contrast, negotiate. It's a whole thing. Ultimately, we default upon the simplest lamp there: a straight rod with a shaded bulb at the top. Done.

We buy it, go back to my place. I put the lamp together...make a new spot of glow in the apartment. It hurts and makes me squinty.

Mom says, "Much better. And you know, you can pin those blankets back, let a little more light in here, really change the feel of the place."

I sigh, rub my eyes...mentally organize liquor store options again.

Eventually, they leave. I disassemble the lamp, box it, pitch it into the closet.

I put it back together one year later when my parents visit again.

They look around, say, "Hey, you still have the lamp!"

I say, "Yes!"

We sit, stare, fake smile, wait out the awkwardness. They leave. I box up the lamp, pitch it in the closet for another year.

ह๑

Beekeeper

2006

I.

After I meet with a psychologist for a few sessions, she begins to mention the possibility of an autism spectrum diagnosis. I bristle, insist I'm just there to talk about depression.

She asks if I'm familiar with the autism spectrum.

I tell her, "I guess I don't want to talk about labels or diagnoses or any of that. I don't know if I trust in stuff like that, overall."

She asks, "You don't know if you trust in what?"

"In...I don't know. Words or whatever. Too much of this stuff just feels like empty words to me."

"We can talk about some of what I'm seeing," she says. "We can talk about the spectrum, what that means. If you have questions and wanted to know more about that, I could help you. But if you're saying that's off the table...then okay."

"It's better to just keep it off the table for now. Until I know if I really want to do this."

She nods. And she keeps her word, steers clear of the topic as the months go by.

After a year or so, I begin to feel a little curious. I mention the spectrum every now and then, say I'd read an article or blog. She always has the same response: "When you're ready to talk about that, tell me, okay? I personally would like that."

I kept getting less and less standoffish about it. One day she says, "You know, a lot of the time when adults receive a spectrum diagnosis...they realize they have a family member who fits the profile. They realize it's not such an out-of-the-blue thing. And that can help them think about it more concretely...that can help come to terms with it, sometimes. I wonder if that could be a first step for us."

I don't say anything. She continues.

"Can you think of any relatives who remind you of yourself? Or have traits that might fit within a spectrum profile?"

"Not really. I don't know."

She holds her hands up, palms out, says, "I'd like to share some observations, but we'll hold off. No pressure, okay?"

She waits. I fidget, swat at my shoelaces. I change topics.

II.

A few months later, a family get-together happens. It's at my grandmother's house. There will be aunts, uncles, cousins, the whole thing; a few dozen people. Because I've been social-hiding for quite a few years now, these are people I haven't seen in a long time.

I go, but can't bring myself to enter the house. I'm too tense with anxiety, so I stroll in big circles around the yard.

This is out in the country, so there are chickens and geese roaming around, a goat pen. I just watch animals, kick rocks, throw pine cones at tree stumps...passing time, waiting it out.

I hear sounds coming from the old workshop in the back yard. I stare at the shop; all of the doors are closed. The sounds can only be Uncle Jay; he's always in the shop. At any get-together or reunion, the first thing he does is seal himself up in the shop and avoid everyone as much as he can. You rarely see him, so I usually even forget he's in there.

He practically lives at my grandmother's house. He sticks around to do the chores she can't—with the garden, with the animals, and so on—so he's always there. But during social events, he does the hiding thing in the shop.

His hiding has never bothered me at all, but a lot of the family think of him as strange. He's an introvert to the point that most people call him a hermit. In a small town like this, it's not an okay way to be. It comes off as rude to some, weird to others.

I think about that.

I walk over to the shop, knock a few times. I hear him grunt the word, "Yup." Nothing else. To the closed door I say, "Just wanted to...I don't know, really. Thought I'd say hi."

It's quiet for ten seconds, twenty. Then thirty. Then I hear a quiet, "Hello."

Nothing else.

I open the door, step into the shop. It's a grimy old workshop filled with benches and saws and metal bins. Tools are piled and stacked up everywhere. Uncle Jay is sitting at one table, staring at a heap of machine parts. He's gifted with whatever it's called when you can take things apart, fix them, put them back together. Like his father, he loves old machines, their bits and pieces, how they work together. I just assume that's why he's in the shop so much, building, disassembling, fixing, tinkering.

This is a small, rural community and he's basically the town handyman. When something breaks down—lawnmowers, cars, etc.—people ask him for help. And he does help, but always at random, unexpected times. He waits until no one is around before fixing anything. Usually he waits until people go to work before showing up at their house, but he's also been known to make repairs in the middle of the night, when everyone is asleep, just to avoid the interaction. People just wake up, find their lawnmower in a conspicuous place, suddenly working.

I look around the shop, find a bench to sit on. He doesn't move. He just sits perfectly still, staring off into space. I ask how he's doing.

He opens his mouth. Closes it. It's quiet for ten seconds, twenty. Then thirty. Then he says, "Oh. I'm good."

I nod. For awhile we just sit, stewing in the awkward silence. I point at the machine bits in front of him, ask what he's working on.

He laughs and says, "Alternator. I had a sort of funny idea."

When I ask about the idea, he just laughs again, doesn't say anything else, so we go back to the silence.

I try a few other topics. He responds with monosyllabic grunts.

Then I say, "Outside, I noticed the stack of boxes. Is that for bees?"

"Yes," he replies. "Been keeping bees for probably two years now. Oh, bees are interesting."

I ask if he's getting honey. His entire demeanor changes. He sits up straight, turns around to face me. He starts waving his hands around and says, "You wouldn't believe the honey! It's...I thought you just get bees, start making honey. But it's...oh it's so interesting."

He stands up, starts digging through a few cabinets, says, "You gotta see this."

He walks over to me, shows me a small ventilated box. He asks, "Do you know what this is?"

I shake my head no.

He says, "So what happened is that, one time, I saw this ad in a magazine. And it said, send us some money *and we will mail you a queen bee!*"

He sits down, shakes his head in disbelief. "Well, I had to find out if that was real, so I sent the money. And one day this box here just shows up in the mail. So I open it and there's this bee just sitting there, looking at me. And I just stood there, looking at her. I couldn't believe it. Someone mailed me a queen bee. So I ran to the library and started researching bees, because I had no idea what to do with her."

I laugh. He gets up again, starts taking books out of a cabinet, says, "I ended up buying these. You wouldn't believe how many bee books are out there."

He stacks around a dozen books on the table.

"You read all of those?" I ask.

He says, "Oh I had to. I had to take care of her, you know. It turns out bees are complicated and you have to really understand them to make them comfortable."

He starts leafing through a book, says, "So, to start a colony, you don't need a ton of bees or honey or any of that. All you have to do is get the queen bee and set her up in the right kind of box. Then, bees from the area will just show up to start working for her. That's how I got started."

He proceeds to describe the honey collection process. He says that if you take too much honey at once, the bees lose interest, leave the hive. He says the trick is to take just the right amount each time, and to make sure they have plenty of honey developed before you even attempt a first harvest.

Then he discusses bee behavior. And hive construction. And brood chambers, mite infestations, odor plumes. He describes (with bonus demonstrations) the various tools you need to maintain a hive.

He talks for forty straight minutes. Then he pauses, stares at the small, ventilated box and says, "The day she showed up. In a box. I'll never forget that."

Then he's silent.

I sit around a bit longer, try to renew the conversation, but he just sits and stares. It's like the words emptied out of him, hourglass style.

I get up to leave. At the door I tell him, "Thanks for the discussion." He nods, doesn't say anything.

I walk away, decide to go home.

Later that day, I tell mom that I had a conversation with her brother. She replies, "He doesn't talk much, but when he does, he can really go on."

I describe his beekeeping set-up.

"Most people don't know it," she says, "but he has all sorts of hobbies. Once he gets settled on something, he goes all in. Did he show you the pictures?"

"No. What pictures?"

"He takes close-up pictures of rocks. He goes into the woods with a camera, takes pictures, develops them, then sorts them."

"How does he sort them? Like, what specifically interests him about rocks?"

"I have no idea. He won't talk about it. He just showed me the pictures one day. He has thousands of them. He had a cabinet filled with thousands and thousands of pictures of rocks."

III.

A week later, the psychologist asks how I'm doing. I nod. She says, "So, you had a family thing over the weekend? How was it?"

I think about it.

It's quiet for ten seconds, twenty. Then thirty.

"Uneventful," I tell her.

Hiding is a difficult habit to break.

ॐ

Oubliette

I.

When I was in elementary school, my social struggles developed into an intense fear of other people.

I sought out friendships, connections, but lacked the standard communication skills necessary to traverse the social world. I didn't know that I lacked body language and couldn't see it in others. Needing people, interested in friendship, I repeatedly jumped into interactions, only to stumble for reasons I had no way of understanding.

My self-confidence eroded. I became quiet, withdrawn. That fear-of-other-people thing happened, got hold of me.

II.

In a strange way, the situation improved once the social world became more complicated.

Junior high rolled around. Groups began to coalesce; cliques began to form...forces predicated on the concept of exclusion. The various groups defined themselves by rejecting others. And I was fine with that. Rejection, being kept away from interactions: I found this to be an enormous relief. I was ready to be alone. I wanted to avoid people as much as possible. So I had this unspoken compromise going on at school: groups kept me out; I kept to myself. It was a pretty good system. I just walked around, lost in my head, adrift in a solitude that increasingly felt like a safe, non-threatening alternative to the chaos of others.

III.

Church was a different story. Church should have been the safer place. But beginning in junior high, it became a nightmare. My parents were strong proponents of church life. We attended three times a week, twice on some of those days. Socially speaking? Church doesn't work compromises. Church brings people together, forges bonds. Actively, intensely. Church makes projects of people like me, of the odd, the introverts.

The primary issue was my age: many churches place teens in a youth group. You couldn't escape them. And there is no alternative to the youth group. All of your classes and activities are structured around this group. And the pressure there is to include...a pressure that never lets up. Sunday morning; Sunday night; Wednesday night: there was one class for the teens; and during any church service, all of the youth sat in a section of pews reserved just for them. It was constant, all-encompassing togetherness.

The intentions were good. The goal was to foster a sense of belonging, of connection. I kept asking myself, "I've wanted connection, right?"

IV.

Even in this environment, where meshing was mandatory, I couldn't swing it. I was too clumsy-headed to make friends and navigate even basic conversations.

The pressure to socialize was painful and quite often humiliating. Before Sunday school, the other teens would stand around, talk. I'd stand on the periphery, listening, staring at my feet. People would politely talk to me; I would throw out scripted lines...memorized bits of social dialog. I would make eye contact, count to three, look away. The conversation would die off. I'd go back to staring at my feet.

Internally, I felt broken and lonely and anxious.

V.

It was at this time, at church, that I began to hide.

I put a lot of mental power into developing elaborate escape routines. I was like a social Houdini. Sometimes I would walk away from the groups, hide out in a bathroom stall for awhile (minutes at least, hours if I could get away with it). Sometimes I would find empty Sunday school classrooms. I'd slip into those, keep the lights off; I'd lay sideways on a row of chairs, try to slow my breathing, quiet my thoughts.

Sometimes in these classrooms, I'd stand on a chair, lift a ceiling tile, then climb up, into the mess of beams and pipes above the room. You could pull this off if you climbed on top of a wall, which provided support. I'd scramble up there, then lower the tile and lay along the top of the wall, letting the absolute lack of others radiate comfort into my frazzled body.

That was a favorite place: up, out of my oubliette...hidden in the ceiling, in the darkness. Other people—the ones below—just sounded like echoes, then, much further away. I'd close my eyes, pretend they were old, fading ghosts.

Red Ledger

November, 2011

I.

A family member is getting married. My partner Sarah and I fly in to attend the ceremony. Usually I skip these things, but I'm slowly making an effort to reconnect with people.

Friday night, I go to the rehearsal dinner. I'm not in the wedding, but the rehearsal scene is quieter, more low-key than the wedding will be, so I think it's a good time to mingle, meet family. Most of these folks are people I haven't seen in many years; people I've avoided. My heart feels tense.

However, we're there: Sarah, myself, assorted family, a few friends of the two getting married.

We're in an old gym beside the church, where tables and decorations are being set up. People rehearse the ceremony, then for an hour or so we all sit around the gym, eating, talking. I have a hard time knowing what to say, so I mostly listen and nod my head and stare at my plate.

Dad and uncles talk about hunting and guns. Comedic, yet mildly violent, deer camp stories ensue. Sarah listens and smiles politely. She leans over and whispers, "The south really is different."

People laugh and eat and talk a little more. The bride walks over (I'm meeting her for the first time tonight). Walking beside her is the guy who's supposed to do the sound for the wedding; he's just a local guy who works at the church. Sound guy tells everyone that he won't be able to attend the wedding, a family emergency came up. Bride asks if any of us will volunteer to work the sound in his place. Sound guy explains that he can give a quick tutorial, explain how it all works.

It's quiet, no one immediately volunteers. Bride looks around and says, "M. should do it, right? I keep hearing he's the smart one."

I panic a little. I think by "smart one" she means "nerd." And in her mind, "nerd" is synonymous with tech stuff. The problem is that I'm a whole different species of nerd and have no tech skills whatsoever.

Bride looks at me, says, "You can learn the sound system real quick, right?"

I open my mouth, no words come out. Sarah raises a hand, says, "I'm a fast learner. I'll do it." She elbows me, says, "Be right back." She heads off for the tutorial. She returns 20 minutes later and says, "Looks like I'm doing the music for the wedding."

I say, "Wow, you learned it that fast?"

"Meh, not really," she replies. "The guy explained how the sound board worked. To me, it was just a bunch of knobs and buttons and flippy things. I'll manage."

"That's great," I tell her. "The bride...I think she thinks I'm a tech nerd."

Sarah shrugs, says, "Maybe. I just know she said your name and I saw that rabbit/headlight look cross your face. So, you know. Me to the rescue."

We leave the rehearsal, go to a bar. Sarah drinks a little drink. I drink a big drink. She asks, "Are you nervous about seeing more of your family tomorrow?" In response, I cringe and rub my face and radiate discomfort.

II.

The next morning, day of the wedding, Sarah and I stop by my parents' house for coffee.

Dad is on the couch, watching a football game. He watches intensely, eyes never leaving the screen. His arms and shoulders are rigid with excitement. He periodically blurts monosyllables: "Go!" and "Run!" and so on.

At one point, he says, "M.! Check out this replay!" I look over. I just see bulky dudes milling around; a ball flips into the air or something. I can't really tell what's happening.

Sarah whispers, "They just blocked a field goal attempt." I say, "Oh! Nice block!" and my dad says, "Man, that was something else." I give Sarah a thumbs-up.

Mom walks over with some pictures. She shows them to Sarah and says, "Here are some photos of M. when he was little."

One picture is of me on a basketball team. I was seven years old. Mom says, "He used to love sports."

What?

I say, "Mom, I was the worst player on the team. I didn't score a single point the entire season."

She says, "Oh, you had talent, you were just...too polite. You were too much of a gentleman to push your way to the goal."

This is a disturbingly upbeat interpretation of my relationship to childhood sports. I mostly remember a lot of asthma and ridicule and failure.

She shows a few other pictures, mostly me in sports or martial arts. She says, "He just had so much energy when he was little. That changed later on. He went from active to just...I don't know. I'll never understand what happened."

That was crippling depression. But let's pretend it's mysterious. I shrug and say, "Who knows?"

"I bet it was the asthma," mom says. "I think that really slowed you down."

I drink coffee. Mom and Sarah talk. I watch my dad watch football. He roots and blurts. My brother shows up. He collapses into a recliner and glares at everyone. That's his thing. He glares.

Sarah and I leave.

III.

It's around lunch time. Sarah expresses an interest in food specific to the state. She says, "I don't know what people eat here. I'm curious." So we drive to the river district, find a place that specializes in fried food. We get a basket of catfish and frog legs and, as a side, pickled green tomato.

Then we go and get dressed for the wedding. I have to pull the computer out, go on YouTube, and watch an instructional video on how to tie a tie. It's not something I know. I'm coming out of a really long pajama phase. I practice the video stuff and achieve a tie-like effect.

IV.

We go to the church where the wedding will be held. It's the church my grandparents attended for almost 60 years. My grandfather and uncles helped build it. I was last here for my grandmother's funeral just a few years ago.

We show up early so that Sarah can familiarize herself a little more with the sound system. She spends some time looking at knobs and buttons and flippy things and says, "Looks easy enough."

Then family begins to arrive for the wedding. My dad has a whole mess of siblings...all of whom had multiple children, so the gathering is large. I roam around the church lobby. I see uncles, aunts, cousins, my cousin's children.

These are people I've avoided for many years now. People I last saw just prior to an emotional collapse...one that kept me socially isolated for more than a decade.

The sense of lost time, of frayed connections: it hurts in a way that I can't find words for. There's a hollowness to the day; the handshakes and hugs and greetings all feel like cherished old photographs that are too faded to see.

And it's strange...despite my unexplained absence, everyone is exceptionally nice. Everyone is warm and affectionate. It makes me feel guilty. The darker sparrows that inhabit my mind, they start whispering. They start saying that the time I spent away was entirely my fault; that I can't blame a collapse or depression or my family; that it was a choice, the isolation.

It's particularly painful when I see my cousin's children, kids I've never met until now. I see them and feel simultaneously curious and hurt. I want to know what their little minds are like...what toys or cartoons they obsess over...what personality traits they've absorbed from their parents...and which traits are uniquely their own. I feel curious. And knowing that I could have spent time with them, could have spent the previous years getting to know them, it stings. They're just tiny strangers. I don't know them.

I try to push back the sparrows, their self-loathing, and make an effort to mingle. I baby step a few conversations. Then I go hang out with Sarah, at the sound system. She asks, "How's it going out there?" I just pull my hair and say a bunch of curse words.

A few minutes later my mom walks by. Sarah asks her, "Why is everyone sitting at the back of the church? All of the front and center pews are empty." Mom laughs and replies, "It's a Baptist thing. We fill our churches back to front."

The wedding begins. Sarah turns knobs and flips the flippy things and plays through the various songs. Each song signals a different portion of the ceremony. It's all orderly and scripted and brief. A preacher preaches, rings happen, a bride is kissed. Then we go to a different area of the church, the old gym, for the reception.

V.

It's crowded; my heart is twisted up, anxious. Sarah, freed from her sound duties, is now available to meet people. Humans pass by and I'm obligated to make introductions. With family, I can manage this task fairly well. It's more of a problem with friends of the family because, growing up, I was so introverted that I never really got to know any of these people. I look around and realize, with much of the crowd, I've forgotten their names. The introductions will be a problem.

This happens repeatedly: a vaguely familiar face walks up, says, "M.! Good to see you! And who is this?" And then I have to introduce Sarah to someone whose name eludes me. It's pretty awful.

Mostly I try to skim past it. I just say, "This is Sarah!" and leave it at that. A few times, it actually works; the person shakes her hand, offers their own name. A few other times, it fails miserably. I say, "This is Sarah!" And the person waits for me to introduce them as well. So I stand there open-mouthed, stewing in the awkward silence, until the person says their own name. Stiffly, a bit offended. They walk away and I pull my hair and mumble curse words.

Eventually, once I've introduced her, Sarah starts to jump in with, "And you are?", mercifully cutting me out of the process. It works better that way.

One woman walks up and greets Sarah. She says, "I'm friends with his mom going way back. We all grew up together around here. Now, I have to tell you this story. M. may not remember it. When he was, oh, around 5 or so, his parents came over to our place for dinner. M. was with them. They walk in and I tell you what, they practically had to drag M. inside. He just did not want to be around us. Eventually they got him in the house. He was on the couch for a bit, just sitting there looking absolutely miserable. Finally, he got up, ran to the door and started pounding on it. With both fists. And full volume, he yelled, 'Let me out of here!' And I just thought that was the funniest thing. I mean, I felt bad, but the sight of such a little kid pounding on that door...it was something else. I remember that clear as day."

The woman walks away. Sarah says, "I didn't know how to tell her you still do that."

Later, I tell that story to my mom, ask her if she remembers it. She says, "Not really. That happened so often, I just stopped noticing after awhile."

People mingle, make plates, sit around tables, talk and talk. I just pace around the periphery of the reception. I'm too stressed to eat. Sarah makes me a plate anyway, but I don't have an appetite. I just push a strawberry in circles around the plate.

Eventually, I sit. I listen to the sound of nearby conversations. I watch kids dart around the room. I watch my dad tell a story to some of his brothers. He pantomimes shooting a gun, waves his arms around, makes funny faces.

Sarah and I leave for a bit to drive around the old neighborhood. We look at the house I grew up in. My grandmother's former house, where a lot of my family were born and raised. We look at my old elementary school and see the playground, where I got my ass kicked pretty regularly. There's a convenience store down the road from the school...starting in 6th grade I used to sneak away from class, walk to the store, shoplift candy bars.

We drive and drive.

Briefly, we go back to the church, say goodbyes.

VI.

We head back to the hotel. I get a drink in the lobby bar, try to mentally decompress. But conversations from the day replay in a loop. Over and over.

I think mostly about my family and how nice they were...both to me and to Sarah. I think about how uncomfortable I am around them. And it's a common occurrence: when I really examine the discomfort I feel around people, I find—not traits in others I dislike or any rational position upon which to stand—I just find a lot of confusion and self-doubt and uncertainty about my own nature.

Darker sparrows replay it all until my head feels heavy.

ABOUT THE AUTHOR

M. Kelter is a writer from the Ozarks. He blogs autobiographically at Invisible Strings (http://theinvisiblestrings.com/) and is a contributor for the Thinking Person's Guide to Autism.

CYBORGS, LUDDITES, AND TO-DO LIST APPS: AN AUTISTIC USE OF TECHNOLOGY

A.C. BUCHANAN

I get up. My to-do list app reminds me to shower, clean my face and teeth, take any medications and supplements. If there's background noise (like that one neighbour everyone has whose lawnmower is twice as loud as any other and who likes using it at all hours) I slip on a pair of noise-cancelling headphones. If I'll be working in town today, I have another pair in my bag. If I'm working from home I'll maybe instant message a friend before setting a timer to track how much time I spend on each activity.

Much of this is not unusual for a self-employed person in their early thirties. But the extent to which some of these things—especially the to-do list app and noise-cancelling headphones—are essential for me is less typical. As an autistic person, I use technology more than the average person, and for things that most non-disabled or neurotypical people wouldn't even consider. (To be autistically-precise, when I say technology here I'm generally meaning that which uses electricity and some kind of processing unit—laptops, tablets, and the like, along with the software that runs on them—rather than, say, the wheel or a pulley system.) To flesh out and add to the examples I began with:

◆ I have poor spatial awareness and sense of direction, struggle to process verbal directions, and can sometimes "zone out" while walking or on a bus. Before I had a tablet with mobile internet and GPS, I would get badly—and occasionally dangerously—lost on a frequent basis.

◆ Due to my dyspraxia, I can only write a sentence or two by hand without pain and otherwise struggling. My auditory processing is impaired, and while I'm generally verbal, speaking can be hard in times of stress or overload. It's rare that I have to rely on technology for communication, but it's really good to have the option.

◆ Meeting and connecting with people can be hard, not just for the usual autistic reasons, but also because so much of it happens in noisy venues, where I find it difficult to hear. While I know some autistic people hate social media, it's essential to me.

◆ Sensory overload makes concentrating difficult. I use the Bose QC25 noise-cancelling headphones, the gold standard which should, in my opinion, be available on subsidised prescription. (My spare pair of active noise-cancelling headphones has taken the place of an extra bottle of water in our emergency grab and run bag. I figure emergency shelters will be dealing with dehydration before they're dealing with sensory overload.)

◆ My most severe difficulties centre around short term memory and organisation, and this is perhaps where technology helps the most. I use a todo-list application and a connected time-tracking application, along with calendar apps and an extension that allows me to automate the sending and receipt of emails. These are imperfect—and I haven't found a solution that truly works—but I can function in a way I simply wouldn't without them.

None of this is universal, of course—there are autistic people who hate these types of technology, or find them inaccessible. But anecdotally, autistic people—and especially autistic people my age and younger—frequently use technology in somewhat similar ways. We trial both hardware and software, aware that what works for neurotypicals may well not work for us—and vice versa—and once we've found something that helps, we rely on it heavily. We use software in ways it was designed for, and ways it wasn't designed for, and sometimes we make our own.

It's not always a matter of having the most advanced gadget either. Technological improvements and upgrades can create as many problems for disabled people as they solve. The move from text to mouse-based, and more recently touch-screen, input has not always been a benefit for people with impaired motor skills, and touch-screens can also pose problems for those with visual impairment, such as when entering PINs at point of sale. Increased bandwidth availability has increased the tendency to share content by video, often inaccessible to Deaf and visually impaired people. On a personal level, I'm holding out in my use of a separate MP3 player, not only because it's familiar, but also because playing music from my phone or tablet drains the battery, which I'm not good at remembering to recharge.

Little or none of the technology I use is branded "assistive technology" or created primarily with autistic or otherwise disabled people in mind. It's a mixed blessing. On the one hand, I avoid the mark-up in price that comes with anything labelled as for disabled people, and also bypass other barriers to buying—some assistive technology can require medical clearance, or is only available from specific retailers that are particularly inaccessible to autistic people (for example, if you want to buy an item you're advised to "email us"—with little indication of what that email should say). I also avoid some of the stigma that comes with using assistive technology or otherwise being more visibly disabled.

On the other hand, it's harder for me to justify my need to use a commonly-used item. If everyone uses a laptop, people are liable to assume my use of a laptop is just like their use of a laptop, and they struggle to understand why I might need it in a situation where they wouldn't. If I need to advocate for access to technology in a more formal situation—in the workplace or while studying, for example—it's harder for people to see that what for them might be a useful piece of technology, a "nice-to-have," is, for me, a necessary accommodation.

(This is, as an aside, why I'm highly wary of placing excessive weight on the concept of empathy. For people with the majority or more socially acceptable viewpoint—neurotypicals, in this case—it's extremely easy to mistakenly assume others have the same experiences they would have, and to consider that empathy. I'd far rather people listened to, believed, and respected what I tell them about my experiences than have them try—and generally fail—to share my emotional experiences.)

Another result of the technology I need being the same technology other people prefer is that I can be seen as having an unfair advantage when I use it. I'm seen as either having a more enjoyable experience, or being lazy and contributing less work.

This isn't true, much of the time. Often that use of technology only partially allows me to compensate for my impairments. At the same time, however, the idea of technology only being acceptable when it is a need plays into both hierarchies of diagnosis (both in the sense that those with a formal diagnosis are seen as having more valid needs, and that diagnoses of some conditions are seen as more legitimate or equating to more genuine needs than others), and the view that not using technology makes you a better or more authentic person, which I will discuss later. I'm quite happy arguing that, say, I need to type rather than write by hand to an extent that the average person doesn't, but I'd rather argue that anyone should be able to type—or generally use their preferred form of note-taking or communication. Here's why:

Firstly, I was largely undiagnosed as autistic—and otherwise neurodivergent—until I was in my twenties. Some labels were floated, but they either hung around in the background or were rejected. If, say, typing at school was only for people with a particular need to do so, I wouldn't even have seen myself as legitimately having that need, let alone been able to convince anyone with authority that I had it.

It should not be any surprise that ability to obtain a diagnosis correlates with other forms of privilege, most obviously ability to pay, but assumptions about race, gender, and the presence of other impairments or atypicalities, can also affect the chances of getting a correct diagnosis. Requiring a diagnosis or a "circumstance" for access to helpful technology affects otherwise-marginalised people disproportionately.

Secondly, when you start drawing lines, often the people most impacted are the people who sit somewhere around that line. The greatest impact isn't on those who don't need assistive technology at all, but on those who need it but feel their need isn't great enough (and disabled people are frequently pushed to believe they need or deserve less than they do), or have an atypical diagnosis—or, as above, no diagnosis at all. The dismissal of atypical, or less common, diagnoses is especially relevant around autism and related conditions, where the exact diagnoses received can be different for two people with the same traits. For example, sometimes a separate diagnosis is given for Sensory Processing Disorder whereas in other cases sensory processing atypicalities are considered to be just part of autism, or the question of whether a dyspraxia diagnosis or a nonverbal learning disorder diagnosis is given can depend more on the region than the person being assessed. Further, autistic people often require accommodations more typically associated with other disabilities, such as subtitles, written communication, or particular seating. Requiring a specific diagnosis for an accommodation not only disadvantages those who are unable to obtain one, but rarely takes account of the complexities and nuances of diagnosis. People with invisible or less apparent conditions—like autism is for many, though not all, autistic people—are often disbelieved and made to doubt themselves, and drawing lines just plays into that.

Thirdly, when access to technology is made contingent on having a diagnosed need, it forces people to disclose impairments, and presents their needs as unusual or "special," a deviation from the normal range of human experience. Not everyone wishes to disclose their needs, nor is everyone in a position to do so safely. Even when they are comfortable disclosing, requiring a diagnosis or a specific reason reinforces the idea that there are some normal ways of being, and some that you have to have a name and a reason for, making use feel not only inferior for existing as autistic people, but like we need permission or an excuse to be ourselves.

My needs may be statistically less common, absolutely, and I understand that that may mean people are less familiar with them, or need to ask questions to better understand them. But I want a world where we all use the tools that work best for us and have the autonomy to make those decisions, and where disabled people are just choosing the most appropriate tool in the same way as everyone else is.

As an "older millennial," born in the mid-eighties, I feel sometimes like I'm sitting on a border, from neither one world nor the other. I grew up with computers but there's no way I'd consider myself a "digital native"; I had some internet access throughout my teens but it was slow, unreliable, and often restricted, and I couldn't assume others had access to it either. I had a cellphone from the age of fourteen, but it had a monochrome display and certainly wasn't usable for internet access even if I had been able to afford it.

And while to some extent it's an experience that applies to everyone, to see the development of technology over their lifetime, it's something that I think holds a particular emotional component for those born at the time I was. On the one hand, I'm lucky to be where I am now. I'm not sure I'd be able to take basic care of myself—let alone work—in a pre-computer age. My experiences as a teenager and as a younger adult without, for example, mobile internet, make it very apparent how much harder my life would have been had technology not changed in the way it did while I was still relatively young.

Yet on the other, it's very, very apparent to me that some of the circumstances that most restricted my abilities, and even caused me physical pain, needn't have happened, and in fact probably wouldn't have happened had I been born five to ten years later. This wasn't just because technology can adjust or help me compensate for processes I struggle with, but also technology can provide the interpersonal connections I was denied as an autistic, queer teenager living in an isolated environment.

It's also emphasised to me just how socially constructed disability is. It's not just that I was hypothetically more disabled in one environment—in this case a time period—but that it was my actual experience. While I undoubtedly struggle with some things—and will continue to do so with or without any technology currently conceivable—the level to which those things impact my life and exclude me from experiences is highly variable.

I want to say a little about the judgement I've both experienced and witnessed when using technology that serves as assistive technology for me. This judgement, or ableism, takes on a particular form. While some uses of assistive technology may be more likely to elicit ableism in the form of either pity or outright abuse, this form is subtler and ultimately dehumanising. Rather than being seen as people using technology, our use of technology is perceived as undermining our humanity. Rather than seeing use of technology for communication, they perceive me as substituting technology for communication. In their view, technology doesn't aid interpersonal processes, it destroys them.

And so people tell me that handwritten notes are more personal, or that if I'm looking at my phone I'm not paying attention to them (while apparently using all my resources to maintain eye contact at the expense of actually paying attention makes them feel better). When I ordered a custom stamp of my signature, to alleviate the stress and pain of book signings, more than one person—and not even the people I was closest to—practically begged me to still pen-sign books specially for them.

It's hard, sometimes, to know how to react to something like that. It's certainly possible for me to sign occasional books with a pen—and if there was a compelling reason to do so I would. And when you've already been told, repeatedly, that you're hard to get along with, sticking to your guns seems counter-productive. But the underlying hierarchy—the idea that how I might go about doing something is inherently inferior to the more typical ways of doing so—is dismissive, even dehumanising. This hierarchy means that it is assumed to be appropriate for a neurotypical person to request or even require me to experience pain or inconvenience to give them the satisfaction of knowing that a task has been done in the way they prefer.

But there's something more to it than this. It's not just that people consider how I do things—and in particular my use of technology—to be inferior. It's that they specifically associate it with certain undesirable personality traits. Because I press keys on a keyboard rather than moving a pen across a piece of paper, apparently I love the person I'm communicating with less. If I wear headphones, I'm anti-social (rather than trying to preserve my mental energy to I can actually talk to and understand the people I'm there to socialise with). If I set up reminders I'm lazy (rather than taking responsibility for my own schedule).

I remember going to the a local food shop and seeing a poster for a World Handwriting Day that promoted the idea that handwriting—rather than typing—was essential for world peace.

This last example may be ridiculous, almost laughable, but they all tie into a wider pattern, and it's a pattern of dehumanisation. The way I do things, the way many autistic and otherwise disabled people do things, is coded as cold, impersonal, uncaring, lacking in effort—and as we're often already perceived in lacking in emotion or the ability to care about others, it's a double blow. And because, like many disabled people, I've been held to a higher standard than the average person specifically in the areas I find most difficult, the steps I take to manage my impairments and function in this world come with a double edged sword.

Another way people react to my use of technology is to proclaim their differences, that they dislike or struggle to use the technology I do. Valid experiences and opinions, certainly, though they're often expressed with a surprising vehemence, as if my use is an affront to them.

Sometimes they call themselves luddites. It's a word that has entered common parlance to mean one who shuns or opposes recent technology. But the actual Luddites—the disparate groups of textile workers who destroyed machinery in nineteenth century England—hold surprising resonance for me in my relationship with technology.

The original Luddite—or at least the man from whom they took their name—was a young, disabled (the records say "feeble-minded" which could mean any one of a number of things in more modern terms) man named Ned Ludd. He was said to have destroyed machinery perhaps in a fit of rage, perhaps in reaction to either taunt-ing or directions issued by his boss. (Was this anger actually a mis-interpreted meltdown? Was he actually unable to cope with the noise and continuous movement of a factory? We can't know.)

The groups that came after him, however, were reacting to indus-trialisation, and in particular the destruction of their cottage weaving and spinning industries. Mass production had destroyed their ability to earn a living, and their way of life, leaving many with few options but to move to the cities and accept hardship, poverty, and dangerous working conditions.

Their decision to destroy machines has been viewed as stemming from hatred of those machines, and of technology generally. In real-ity, the Luddites had few options available to them. All women and most men—especially working class men—were denied the right to vote. A strike, without legal protections and in a situation where there was an influx of potential workers from rural areas, would have been unlikely to yield results. Perhaps some Luddites did destroy machines because they hated the advancement of technology, but for most it was the only option for resistance in a world where every other path was closed.

When I think of the Luddites, I don't think about hating technol-ogy. I think of being forced to be in an overloading environment, one in which I have no control over the use of technology, where it is designed without any consideration for my needs. I think of having obvious options for resistance, even for communication, taken away from me. I think about longing for the relative quiet of my own cot-tage, far from anywhere, with the technology that I'm used to, that I can adapt for my needs and repair when it goes wrong. (I say relative quiet because I concede the point that there were likely also half a dozen children and probably the odd farm animal in that cottage—I don't want to paint this scenario as idyllic.)

And I think that sometimes words don't mean what we always expect them to mean, that it's so hard sometimes to find the words to describe our experiences, and that sometimes we can find resonance with those experiences in places and times that are not our own.

It's a well worn trope that autistic people are like robots, or identify themselves with them. Often it's an offensive stereotype, used to imply that we have no feelings or personality, or used because they are over-reading physical signs such as speech tone or gait. Sometimes it's a negative self-identification, because we simply haven't been told there are people like us, and believe that we fail as people, and that being a successful robot is a pleasanter alternative to being a failed person.

But sometimes it's not a negative perception of us, or a negative self-identification. Sometimes it's part of how we understand ourselves.

I've written in this essay about often using the same technology neurotypical and non-disabled people do, but in different ways. This has mainly meant using it more frequently, having a need to use it rather than a simple preference, and perhaps using it for things others would not (for example, many neurotypical people may add project-related tasks to a to-do list, but don't need a system to remind them to clean their teeth).

But sometimes I feel I relate to technology in wholly different ways.

It's hard. We spend so much time trying to explain ourselves to neurotypicals—who rarely reciprocate—trying to say that we're really just like you as an attempt to claim our humanity. The effort we put into that can leave us unable to talk or even think about our cultural touchstones, about the ways we think of ourselves.

I said earlier that people sometimes see our use of technology to aid social interaction as us substituting technology for social interaction. I argued that using technology means I can engage in social interaction better, and for longer. I stand by that argument. But technology is more to me than just a tool. And I'm not alone in seeing my autistic experience as inherently connected to technology, in seeing the dividing lines between self and tools as sometimes indistinct. I'm not alone, either, in feeling an affinity to representations of cyborgs, beings whose bodies comprise both organic (e.g. flesh and bone) and biomechatronic (e.g. electronic and metal) components. Even though technology is not integrated with my body in any way that would afford that description—and, indeed, the integration depicted in most (but not all) representations is not yet possible—my use of technology is integral to my sense of self. Fictional depictions of those whose abilities aren't typical, whose humanity is doubted by those around them, and who don't experience their use of technology as a deficiency or an inferior option resonate with me on multiple levels.

In what has until relatively recently been a glaring absence of overt autistic representation—both real and fictional—it's no accident that many autistic people have found resonance in portrayals of artificial humans and electronic beings. Our own—more subtle—technology use forms bonds and becomes the subject of self-deprecating jokes. But the links to our autism aren't always clearly drawn. I feel technology—both the idea of using technology, and the idea of, on some level, being technology—is a crucial part of any understanding of autistic culture, but no aspect of this discussion is easy to define.

So I'm raising a question rather than answering one, trying to contribute to a discussion rather than conclude one. I want to ask the questions about autism and technology that are beyond the obvious topics of "how does technology help you" or "are all autistic people good with computers." I want to ask: how do we see ourselves and how does that relate to technology? How can we discuss our relationship with technology outside of the frameworks created by neurotypical understandings? How do we understand autistic culture, and what role does technology play in that? There will be many different answers—and that's a good thing.

Tonight I went out for a drink with a friend I met on Facebook. I got home without incident mostly due to real-time bus information, and the knowledge I had GPS to rely on—and I wore headphones on the bus home. The fish tank light goes off on a timer, not reliant on my memory. There are emails sitting in a folder ready to go out the next morning; I use an extension that both allows me some time to catch mistakes and sends them on a more typical-person schedule.

The extent to which technology is integrated into my life is, at this point, natural and routine. This is, of course, only one perspective, only one experience; in particular, some autistic people find this type of technology very hard to access, and those perspectives need to be heard as well. But for myself and many other autistic people, our relationship with technology is positive, necessary, and integral to our being—and it needs to not just be accommodated but recognised as an (but not the) experience of autistic culture.

ABOUT THE AUTHOR

A.C. Buchanan is an autistic and dyspraxic human, a web developer, and a science fiction and fantasy writer, located near Wellington, Aotearoa New Zealand. They're the author of several novellas, and their short fiction has been published in anthologies from Paper Road Press, FutureFire.net and Crossed Genres. They also edit Capricious magazine, and like cheese, dinosaurs, and good disability representation in SFF. Their website is at http://www.acbuchanan.org/.

RECOMMENDED RESOURCES

Kit Mead's autism resources webpage (https://kpagination. wordpress.com/autism-resources/) has links to many great resources, including ones on autistic culture, diagnosis, and coping with daily life. It also includes a section for people new to the autistic community and a section for non-autistic allies.

#AutChat is a Twitter hashtag and series of weekly chats for autistic people and autistic cousins, founded in February 2015; the editor of this anthology is a moderator. You can see upcoming topics, past topics and transcripts, and information on how to join chats on the website, http://autchat.com, or check out the #AutChat hashtag on Twitter. #AutChat welcomes people who are formally diagnosed, self-diagnosed, or questioning whether they are autistic.

The Autistic Self Advocacy Network (http://autisticadvocacy. org/) is a U.S.-based disability rights organization run by and for autistic people. They focus on public policy advocacy, autistic cultural activities, and leadership trainings for self-advocates. They also publish books and resources (including this anthology) and have self-advocate-led affiliate groups in various cities, mostly in the U.S. but a few in other countries as well.

The Thinking Person's Guide to Autism (http://www. thinkingautismguide.com/) is a resource "for carefully curated, evidence-based information from autism parents, autistics, and autism professionals." They also have an active Facebook community open to autistic people, professionals, and parents.

CPSIA information can be obtained
at www.ICGtesting.com
Printed in the USA
BVHW091406251120
593999BV00007B/609

9 781938 800078